UNDERSTANDING CAT BEHAVIOR

UNDERSTANDING
CAT BEHAVIOR

A COMPASSIONATE GUIDE
TO TRAINING
AND COMMUNICATION

BETH PASEK

ROCKRIDGE
PRESS

Interior and Cover Designer: Elizabeth Zuhl
Art Producer: Megan Baggott
Editor: Brian Sweeting
Production Editor: Mia Moran

Cover photograph by Shaina Fishman
Interior photographs: ii, 8, 9, 25, 26, 48, 58, 72, 82, 89, 90, 124: iStock; vi: Laura Stolfi/ Stocksy United; x: Jaromir Chalabala/Shutterstock; 14: Melanie DeFazio/Stocksy United; 38: Samantha Gehrmann/Stocksy United; 108: Jovana Rikalo/Stocksy United
Author photo courtesy of Greg Murray Photography

ISBN: Print 978-1-64739-614-5 | eBook 978-1-64739-384-7
R0

THIS BOOK IS DEDICATED TO THE
MEMORY OF TILEI, THE LITTLE DEMON
CAT THAT STARTED MY JOURNEY INTO
UNDERSTANDING CAT BEHAVIOR.

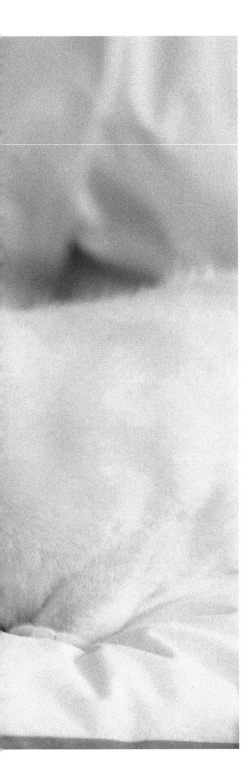

CONTENTS

INTRODUCTION

Welcome, and thank you for making the commitment to learn more about your cat. Whether you're a new cat owner or have had cats your entire life, this book will give you a deeper understanding of why your cats do what they do and what you can do to manage their behavior.

Cat behavior science is a relatively new field, and there are breakthroughs all the time. Sometimes what we thought was true yesterday may not be as accurate as what we learn today. Moreover, cats like to change the rules. But certain basics remain the same. In this book, we will look at some of those basics and show you how to use an understanding of cat behavior to give your cats their best life.

CAT OWNER TO CAT CONSULTANT

As a seasoned cat foster, professional cat sitter, and cat consultant with the International Association of Animal Behavior Consultants-Cat Division, I have a lifelong dedication to improving cats' lives. I have worked with cats of all ages, temperaments, and health statuses for more than 25 years. My company has gone from being a dog walking/pet sitting company to a cat-only company with "pet sitters who speak meow."

I got involved in cat behavior 25 years ago, long before it was even a topic. At that time there was a lot of misleading and inaccurate information out there on dealing with problematic cat behavior.

The first cat I owned as an adult started out as a cat from hell. Tilei was prone to redirected aggression, and I spent many of our days together nursing claw and bite marks. She even put me in the emergency room one night for a bad bite.

After that night, I spoke with my veterinarian. His advice at the time would draw gasps of horror in light of what we know today.

I knew there had to be a better way, so I set out on a mission to make Tilei's life and mine better, safer, and happier. That decision would change the way that veterinarians would come to treat the tiny tiger I brought to their office.

Even today, reference guides for cat owners are relatively nonexistent, and much of the work on training domestic animals has been done with dogs. But cats don't take kindly to the balanced training that works with dogs. I soon realized that positive reinforcement of desired behavior had far better results.

Two publications were instrumental in shaping my observational skills and helping to mold my training style: *On Behavior: Essays and Research* by Karen Pryor, and *The Cat's Mind* by Dr. Bruce Fogle. Together, those early writings helped me gain a deeper understanding of cat behavior.

This journey has taken me from novice cat owner to professional cat consultant, helping cat owners find solutions to cat behaviors that disrupt their lives. I hope this book serves as a resource for you when problem behaviors crop up. Dealing with those behaviors before they get out of hand is far, far easier than letting your cat learn and adopt bad kitty etiquette in the home.

CHAPTER ONE

THE BASICS OF CAT BEHAVIOR

Cats have inspired love and hate, and they were once treated as gods. The mystery of their evolution and the brilliant mutual relationship we've shared for thousands of years has led us to the modern cat we adore.

Only recently has it become understood that the cat has lived with humans much longer than the dog. This makes for a mysterious and fascinating exploration of understanding cat behavior in today's modern cultures. In this chapter, we will explore body language, cat sounds, and behavior at different stages of life. We will look at where the domestic cat came from, how man has exploited this relationship, and how the domestic house cat of today developed. We will also look at some of the very real differences between cats and dogs, breeds of cats, and even between sexes.

THE FUNDAMENTALS OF CAT BEHAVIOR

To understand cat behavior, we need to look at how cats have evolved, how they think, and how they perceive the world around them. We know dogs were domesticated for hunting, protection, and companionship. But how did cats come to associate with humans? In fact, have we ever truly domesticated them at all?

The Evolution of Cats

The way cats evolved is as mysterious as cats themselves. The modern cat is genetically related to a small African cat called *Felis silvestris lybica*, which is a different branch of the evolutionary tree from lions, tigers, and other big cats.

The discovery in Cyprus in 2004 of a cat entombed with its owner was our first indication that small cats were being domesticated approximately 9,500 years ago. As humans began living in agricultural societies, densely populated living quarters attracted rodents, which in turn could have attracted small wild cats. It wasn't long before cats were being used to control vermin where grain was stored and on ships, carrying cats around the world.

The Domestication of Cats

It seems that the cat more or less selected us as a companion. For centuries, cats remained working animals on small farms, cities, and ships. In the Middle Ages, cats were treated as working animals, but due to their friendly nature, they quickly ingratiated themselves to their human masters. In turn, humans favored the friendlier felines. The genetic record shows that by the late Middle Ages, cats were being selected for breeding. It wasn't until the late 18th and 19th centuries that they began to be bred for coat colors and patterns.

Thanks to advances in genetic science, new discoveries are frequently being made. The 2004 discovery of a human and a cat in a mutual burial tomb in Cyprus indicates that this cat-human relationship existed well before the ancient Egyptian culture by nearly 4,000 years. It seems clear this small wild cat traveled the world with man for thousands of years, only to end up as the pampered purring cat on your sofa today.

CAT BEHAVIOR BY AGE

Cat behavior is different at several key stages of life. These differences affect a cat's interaction with their humans and with other cats in the household.

Kittens

Kittens form most of their personality within the first seven weeks after birth. It is during this time that breeders, rescues, and owners need to gently handle the kittens and engage them in play with their littermates, humans, and other animals.

Many rescues start adopting out kittens when they are only eight weeks old. This early adoption strategy is understandable because of the number of kittens born during the spring and summer, but unfortunately it is likely not in the cat's best interest. If you choose a kitten in this age range, it is best to adopt a pair of kittens or locate a "kitten kindergarten." This special class for kittens and owners helps socialize kittens until they are about 13 weeks of age. Studies have demonstrated that kittens adopted out too young tend to be more fearful over the course of their lives and in some cases may develop aggressive tendencies.

A great habit to start with kittens is to help them create a positive association with their cat carrier. Kittens enjoy having a warm "nest." I encourage you to start feeding your kittens in their carrier. Also, handle your tiny kitten's paws often and reward them with treats for allowing your touch—particularly helpful when it comes time to trim their nails, which helps control the damage from scratching. Also, have a wide range of people visit and play with your kitten, and if possible, help your kitten become used to dogs and other species of animals in your home. This desensitization work will help your very young kitten grow into a confident cat.

Adolescent Cats

Unlike dogs, which have a longer socialization period, cats enter adolescence around 13 weeks old. If your kitten wasn't spayed or neutered, this is the time to do so to prevent wandering and other territorial behaviors.

At this age, many of your kitten's personality traits are set for life. Your kitten will start to test boundaries and become more independent, so you need to be sure your home is properly kitten-proofed—being nearly an adult cat, their independent, curious nature guarantees that they can and will get into a fair amount of trouble. Getting stuck in a closet all day is no fun, and as one pet sitter told me, "A cat stuck under the kitchen cabinetry led to a not so wonderful rescue with an electric saw." The kitten was retrieved unharmed but was likely traumatized for life.

Adult Cats

Cats are considered mature adults from approximately two to eight years old. During this time, they continue learning and establishing the social order around them. Cat social order is fluid and can change from day to day, affecting which cat uses which litter box or which one gets to sit at the top of the cat tree. Minor spats are common, although all-out fights between cats need to be addressed in terms of establishing adequate territory and ensuring access to resources.

While they may not be as active as kittens, your adult cats still need mental and physical enrichment in their environment. Socialization continues, but at a much slower and more cautious pace. Cats in this age group are well served by you continuing to create an enriched environment using cat trees, play, food puzzles, and training.

Senior Cats

I must admit that senior cats, those over eight years old, are my favorites. But older cats come with their own behaviors, and many owners do not have a good understanding of their senior cat's needs and how aging affects their overall health and mental well-being. Senior cats may need help with grooming, getting up on the sofa or bed, and going up or down stairs. Age-related issues are often the number one reason I get calls about behavior.

You need to take your senior cats to the veterinarian several times a year. At these visits, tell your veterinarian about any behavior changes, such as:

» No longer climbing the cat tree
» Using the basement litter box less frequently
» No longer jumping onto the sofa or bed
» Showing significantly reduced play or activity levels
» Suddenly displaying more needy behavior
» Leaving larger than normal urine clumps in the litter box
» Showing increased thirst
» Meowing all night
» Failing to use the litter box

All these changes in behavior may indicate an underlying health condition that needs attention. Only once the medical condition is dealt with, whether it be a minor bacterial infection or something more serious, can any sort of behavior modification begin.

CAT BEHAVIOR BY SEX

Almost all domesticated animals are castrated or "fixed." Companion animals like cats and dogs benefit from having this completed before sexual maturity. There are significant differences between males and females as well as between unneutered and neutered animals.

Male and Female Cats

Male cats who remain unneutered will show signs of territorial wandering, fighting, aggression, and marking behavior (spraying). They can be more vocal, destructive, and in some cases less hygienic. These issues can present significant challenges. If you want your male cats to look like male cats and have the secondary male characteristics like a thick neck and more pronounced muscles, I encourage you to neuter them as soon as practical after they develop those secondary features. Doing so will diminish the development of unwanted habits.

Female cats who are not spayed may mark territory in a similar fashion to a tomcat. You will find them trying to apply urine to vertical surfaces and, if they can't, climbing up and urinating on elevated surfaces. They will also be more vocal and likely to present you with their pelvis when they are in heat. Even if you keep your cat indoors, she may attract unwanted male visitors through her plaintive calls, resulting in the outside of your home smelling like tomcat urine, cat fights in your yard, and the sounds of cats calling each other at all hours.

Spaying and Neutering

One of the first questions a cat behavior consultant will ask is whether your cat is spayed or neutered. If the cat is not yet "fixed," you will be encouraged to have the procedure completed. The procedure often reduces several of the undesired behaviors and may decrease the intensity of others.

Spaying and neutering reduce the risk of disease and extend your cat's life. According to the ASPCA, spaying a female cat significantly reduces her risk of mammary cancer. The procedure is also vital for controlling the cat population. If you have ever volunteered with a rescue during the spring and summer, you know that the number of kittens needing to find homes is astronomical. Many kittens never get to rescue because there simply is no room. There is no logical reason not to spay or neuter your cat, considering the benefits to the cat and to help combat the problem of cat overpopulation.

CAT CHRONICLES:
HARRIS THE MISUNDERSTOOD CAT

Fear, anxiety, and stress can be interpreted as aggression. Jannel often travels for work, and this past month she needed to take at least one extended trip. But after Jannel's longer trip, Harris started showing signs of agitation with the cat sitter.

Jannel had hired one of our cat sitters to spend one hour a day with the cats, engaging them in petting, play, or whatever fancy the cats had for that day.

The time for the sitter to leave approached, and she placed a few treats within the cat toys, which Harris began to investigate. The cat sitter pulled out her phone and recorded the events that followed. When the alarm started to beep, Harris lay down in front of the cat sitter to block the exit door. He was swatting and hissing, clearly telling the cat sitter, "Don't leave me."

Most people don't recognize separation anxiety in their cat. In fact, many people would consider Harris to be a nasty cat. But Harris was very lucky to have one of our cat sitters trained to recognize anxiety. We sent the video showing Harris's behavior to Jannel, his owner. To make sure that Harris's issue wasn't medical, we asked Jannel to have Harris seen by the vet and to share the video with him.

Jannel's vet prescribed an over-the-counter dietary calming supplement coupled with our proposed behavior modification plan: The alarm was set to silent mode so no beeping would sound when the sitter was ready to leave. Two combinations of plug-in pheromone diffusers were used. Visits were no longer to be an hour long but split into two separate visits, with the evening cat sit visit being longer. Calming cat music was left playing for up to 15 hours overnight when Jannel was away. The dietary calming supplement was given in the morning.

These changes in how Harris's environment was managed while his owner was out of town made a significant impact on his behavior. His owner's next long trip resulted in a peaceful environment, great visits with his cat sitter, and a clearly happy cat.

CAT BEHAVIOR BY BREED

Cat shows are both beauty pageant and contest. Here in Cleveland, the cat show is a big deal. For the past several years we have had the pleasure of hosting the Cat Fanciers' Association International Cat Show at the IX Center. This show brings the very best of all the breeds of cat together for one spectacular weekend in what is recognized as the largest cat show in the United States. I personally attend two to three local shows throughout the year (one to see the stunning beauty of a purebred cat and the other to obtain the highly prized toys for my cat behavior business). Alliance, Ohio, just outside of Cleveland, is home to the Cat Fanciers' Association and the Feline Historical Museum.

Purebred cats are less common than purebred dogs. Purebred cats make up only about 7 percent of the overall cat population. There is a strong likelihood the cats you have are no specific breed, even if you obtained them through a breed-specific rescue.

While we see dogs bred for certain jobs like hunting, protection, and companionship, cats are bred for their looks, and many have desirable temperaments and traits that endear them to the owners who love them.

There are 45 breeds of cat recognized by the Cat Fanciers' Association. I am not going to list them all here, but I will go over a few of the more popular breeds that have significant behavior needs. You can find more information at cfa.org/breeds or at your local cat show.

BENGAL CAT: This breed of cat isn't allowed in the show ring until after the fourth generation of breeding. Bengal cats are a cross with the small Asian Leopard Cat. This cat can win you over on looks alone. But don't be deceived: This cat is highly active and curious, and quickly learns to do tricks. As such, kittenhood with these cats can prove a true challenge for a new cat owner. They keep their athleticism well into their senior cat years.

MAINE COON: This is one of America's most loved breeds and for great reasons. The Maine Coon is America's native long-haired cat. This breed is large, with male cats topping out often over 20 pounds. These lovable giants of the cat world are typically laid-back and highly intelligent. They are often described as "dog-like."

PERSIAN: Another popular breed of long-haired cat, Persians are small cats with a great temperament who prefer a home that is secure and serene. This cat is not prone to jumping or climbing.

SIAMESE: Known to be chatty and demanding, Siamese cats are recognized for their intelligence and loving nature. They are one of what the cat world calls true "people cats."

AMERICAN SHORTHAIR: The American Shorthair is a lovely family cat. With their sweet and easygoing disposition, they often make a wonderful first cat for children to experience. The American Shorthair is one of the oldest recognized pedigreed cats.

CAT BEHAVIOR VS. DOG BEHAVIOR

Many people are confused by cat behavior because of the misconception that cats followed the same domestication path as dogs. But the cat's path from small wild cat to pampered house cat is incredibly different. Dogs were bred for different jobs, but cats naturally exist in a mutually beneficial relationship with humans. Little attention was paid to cats as we didn't need to

BEHAVIOR	DOG
Group or family mentality	Will need to be involved in everything you do around the home
Bathroom habits	Dogs need several weeks of "housebreaking"
Praise	Dogs enjoy your praise as a reward itself
Treats for training	Definitely need
Belly rubs	Most dogs enjoy these
Door greeting	Dogs will jump, bark, and excitedly greet you at the door
Strangers	Most dogs are excited and willing to meet strangers
Play	Dogs like rambunctious play and may growl, bark, fetch, and enjoy the all-out run
Petting	Most dogs enjoy a good chest rub and pat
Training resilience	Dogs require more rote-style training with repeated exercises

teach them to perform tasks, such as catching rodents. It is only in the last 50 to 100 years that we've begun more seriously thinking about training cats.

Let's look at some of the similarities and differences between cat behavior and dog behavior.

CAT

Will likely notice your activities around the home, but will not be directly involved

Cats learn to use the litter box very quickly

Most cats will look at you without reaction, although with training a cat will acknowledge your praise

Definitely need

Some cats enjoy these whereas others may offer their belly and then latch on in attack mode

If a cat greets you at the door you may get head bunts and perky meows

Cats prefer to observe strangers from a distance and approach when they feel the person is not a threat

Cats enjoy play that most closely mimics hunting behaviors of stalking and pouncing

Cats prefer a gentle scratch around the face, a single finger cheek rub, or a scratch between the shoulder blades

Due to the cat's independent nature, they require shorter training sessions and retain what they've learned longer

INDOOR CATS AND OUTDOOR CATS

Outdoor cats experience all kinds of challenges in their environment. The average male cat (neutered or not) will roam approximately 10 houses in any direction; female cats stay closer to home. Not only are outdoor cats hunters who might occasionally bring home little "gifts" for you, they can also be preyed upon themselves by dogs, coyotes, owls, and other animals. They can be hit by cars, get trapped in machines or small structures, and more. They can also attract parasites such as fleas, ticks, and intestinal worms, some of which are zoonotic, meaning that they can pass them on to you or your children.

Indoor cats, who are safe from these kinds of dangers, have a challenge of their own: boredom, often accompanied by an unhealthy weight gain. That is why an enrichment program for your indoor cats is important. Having perching places so they can look out the windows, cat trees, and several types of toys, as well as spending time interacting with you in play sessions, helps to keep your cats physically healthy and mentally happy.

CATS AS INDIVIDUALS

"Just when you think you know the cat, the cat changes the rules."

—Michael T. Nappier, DVM, DABVP
Assistant Professor, Community Practice
Virginia-Maryland College of Veterinary Medicine

With cats having such a short domestication history but a long-enduring mutual relationship with humans, it is amazing that we don't understand them better. But as we learn more about the roles that genetics, environment, and building bonds play with our cats, we begin to see they are individuals, each as unique as a human being. Some like to cuddle; others would rather sit quietly in the room near you. There's the percher and the den cat—all of them sentient beings that want the companionship of humans. But it's important to remember that each cat's personality is a function of instinct and survival. Projecting human emotions onto the cat only muddles your understanding of their behavior.

CHAPTER TWO

CAT COMMUNICATION

What is your cat saying to you? What are you saying to your cat? Recently, researchers discovered that cats communicate with their human owner in a unique "language," made up of sounds, scent, and body language. Even when they make similar sounds and have similar behaviors as other cats, your cats have their own special way to communicate with you.

CAT NOISES

"Meow" comes in many variations and means something different depending on its tone, length, and intensity. Cat behavior specialists can often distinguish the meaning of the meow, given the context in which it is being used.

MEW: The happy, endearing greeting you might hear when you arrive home.

PLAINTIVE MEOW: Your cat wants something. For example: "Feed me right now."

LONG DRAWN OUT MEOW: This is a demand. For example: "I want to go out NOW."

YOWL: Your cat makes this sound when very upset. It's best to avoid engaging with the cat at this time.

SILENT MEOW: The silent meow is not silent. Your cat is meowing at a level you cannot hear. You can see the cat's mouth move but you will hear no sound.

PURR: You might be surprised to learn this sound is often misunderstood. A happy cat will purr, but so will a cat that is in a great deal of pain or stress. While we still don't understand the mechanisms that allow a cat to purr, we do know that depending on when a cat uses purring, it means different things and, in some cases, can be physically healing for both cat and human. It turns out that a cat's healing purr is in the same vibration range (23 Hz to 125 Hz) as that of a TENS (transcutaneous electrical nerve stimulation) device.

CHIRP OR TRILL: This is considered a sound of happiness that your cat may use while twining around your legs.

CHATTER: Your cat might make this sound when it spots a bird or other prey outside the window. Chatter is considered by many to be a sound of frustration.

HISS: We have all seen a cat hiss at some point. Hissing is an unmistakable sign that your cat is angry.

GROWL: Yes, cats do growl, but at such a low level that you may not recognize that your cat is extremely angry or frightened.

MATING: Mating sounds are a series of loud, persistent meows and yowls. Male cats make mating sounds when they sense a female in heat. In a similar way, females use these sounds to announce themselves as ready for mating. Much of this unpleasant noise can be avoided by neutering or spaying your cats.

CAT FACIAL EXPRESSIONS

Your cat's face is full of expressions, but do you really understand their meanings? A survey done by Georgia Mason, a behavioral biologist at the University of Guelph in Ontario, found that most of us don't read cat facial expressions very well. In fact, out of the 6,000 participants, only 13 percent scored 75 percent or above. Even people who have studied a cat's facial expressions can find them hard to read. Let's get a little better at it here.

Eyes

Your eyesight and your cat's eyesight are as different as night and day. Cats see better in low light conditions than we do, and cats have better peripheral vision by about 20 degrees. We see objects at a distance better than a cat, but cats see things from 3 to 20 feet away with better resolution than we do. If you have ever put a toy right in front of your cat, you may notice that they seem uninterested in it. That's because the cat's vision is poor at that range. Move the toy a few feet out and suddenly you have an engaged and interested cat.

Like your cat's sounds, the eyes can give you clues about what they are feeling.

SLIT PUPILS: Most cats will have slit pupils when they are in a relaxed state or in bright sunlight.

DILATED PUPILS: When your cat is excited or aroused the pupil dilates, opening the eye as a camera does to let more light in and better target the prey or the toy.

HALF-CLOSED EYES: A cat with half-closed eyes is either catnapping or possibly in discomfort.

SLOW BLINK: This behavior has been made famous as the "I love you" blink and is often shared between owner and cat.

AVOIDING EYE CONTACT: The cat is likely distressed and considering a flight response or doesn't want to be bothered.

Ears

Cats have an amazing ability to hear—in fact, they are the mammal with the widest range of hearing, based on findings by Rickye and Henry Heffner in their study *Hearing Range of the Domestic Cat*. They can hear in low ranges like humans and high ranges beyond what most dogs can hear. Cats also have up to 30 muscles in their ears, which gives them the ability to hear in several directions at once. Your cat's ear position can also tell you a lot about how they are feeling in the moment.

ALERT/PERKED EAR: Your cat is focused on something, is likely to be calm, and might be feeling playful.

"AIRPLANE" EARS: Airplane, or flattened, ears indicate that your cat is feeling anxious or stressed. The flatter the ears, the more fearful and likely to attack the cat will be. You need to proceed with caution around a cat like this.

PINNED EARS: Pinned ears indicate that your cat is extremely stressed and is best left alone. This ear position is when their ears are back, appearing pinned to their head. If you're worried, you can put a laundry basket over the cat, then shuttle them to another room and leave them alone to calm down. Check on them after an hour and see if they will take food. If not, close the door and try again every hour or so.

TWITCHY EARS: The anecdotal evidence is that the ear twitch signals direction. For example, when two cats meet, one might signal the amicable way to pass by twitching one ear in a specific direction. Your cat might sit down in front of you near mealtime and twitch its ear toward its food cabinet. If you ignore the signal, your cat might meow at you until you get the message. What amazing creatures we live with!

Whiskers

All the cat owners I know adore their cat's whiskers. These long, beautiful vibrissae are incredible. They contain sensory nerves that the cat uses to add more information about its surroundings and to contribute to its hunting skills. Your cat's whiskers are also another way to communicate with you.

WHISKERS FULL FORWARD: Your cat is interested in the environment, either playing with you or stalking prey.

WHISKERS TO THE SIDE: Your cat is relaxed, resting, and comfortable.

WHISKERS MOVING BACK: Your cat is stressed, anxious, or fearful, so you need to take care. The further back the whiskers are, the more stressed your cat has become.

Pain

A subject not often mentioned when discussing cat expressions is pain. The Feline Grimace Scale is an assessment tool for veterinarians, developed and tested by researchers at the University of Calgary and Montreal, that rates a combination of facial expressions and body language that can indicate if a cat is in pain. For example, in one combination, the cat's face appears winced or flattened, with the whiskers tipped forward and ears slightly flattened and rotated out. It's a very subtle signal, but when combined with the cat's history and assessment, there's a good chance the cat is in pain. This is especially true of senior cats.

CAT CHRONICLES: ARTY THE CAT WHO WANTED TO BE PETTED . . . OR NOT?

Arty would jump up into his owner's lap and deliver a few head bunts to her hand. But when Carol started to pet him, Arty would suddenly turn to deliver a bite. Carol reported that this would happen without warning. Cats rarely bite without warning. Most often, this happens when an owner doesn't know how to read the signals.

As I was sitting with Carol on her sofa, big friendly Arty jumped up next to me and solicited attention. Carol tensed, fearing I would be bitten. As Arty introduced himself with a sniff and head bunt, I noticed that his eyes were already dilated, his whiskers half back and his ears slightly back. I opted to not attempt to pet him and just let him do his thing. After a while, he lay down peacefully next to my leg.

Carol was surprised at what had just happened. She reached out to pet him, but I told her not to. I explained that Arty was aroused by the encounter, and even though he had settled down next to me, his ears and whiskers told me he was still anxious. Petting aggression is one of the behaviors that confuses pet owners. Arty was a good example of what it looks like.

Carol's plan going forward would include learning to recognize Arty's mood, desensitization for Arty in the form of letting him settle down after his greeting, waiting for his ears and whiskers to signal that he had relaxed, and only then giving him a few short pets. Over time, Carol would be able to slowly increase the amount of petting that he tolerated.

Several months later Carol and I did a follow-up. I watched as Arty jumped up and gave her a great big head bunt, then lay down in her lap. Carol smiled as we chatted, and Arty fell contentedly asleep. Carol had learned to read Arty's love language and while his behavior was still not entirely perfect, it was far better than it had been a few short weeks before.

CAT BODY LANGUAGE

We've examined the ways in which cats communicate with their faces. Like humans, cats also communicate their needs and feelings with their body language. It's important to learn what they are saying and not to project human (or canine) body language onto them. Learning cat body language is learning how to understand what they are actually "saying."

Tail

Your cat's tail is a magnificent appendage that helps with balance, posture, and communication. You can use the tail as an indicator of the cat's mood at a given time.

FLAGPOLE TAIL: This is often considered the happy tail, which the cat uses at greetings.

TAIL UP AND QUIVERING: Your cat is really thrilled to see you!

TAIL UP AND QUIVERING (UNNEUTERED CAT): Your cat is spraying and marking territory.

QUESTION MARK TAIL: An endearing tail position that might convey love—or the cat has a question for you. For example, you shook the treat bag and the cat is asking, "Am I getting a treat?"

BOTTLE BRUSH TAIL UP: Your cat is angry.

BOTTLE BRUSH TAIL DOWN: This tail position is a defensive signal that indicates your cat is frightened.

TAIL MIDWAY OUT FROM CAT'S BODY AND TIP CURLED UP: Your cat is relaxed.

SIDE SWISH OF STANDING CAT: Your cat might be feeling amorous—or angry.

SIDE SWISH OF SITTING CAT: Your cat is annoyed.

TAIL TUCKED BETWEEN THE LEGS: Your cat is extremely frightened and anxious.

TAIL WRAPPED AROUND THE BODY: Your cat might be content and relaxed, although taken with facial features this position can also indicate the cat is in pain.

Postures

Like the tail position, your cat's body posture conveys lots of information about how they're feeling.

BELLY UP: Most cat owners know that this is one of the most misinterpreted postures. It generally means that your cat trusts you. Unlike when a dog does this, it is not an invitation to pet the belly.

HALLOWEEN CAT: A cat in the typical arched back, bottle brush tail position is trying to signal you to increase your distance by making itself look taller, bigger, and scarier. Avoid aggression by giving the cat the distance it wants.

CROUCHING CAT: Crouching indicates anxiety: small, tail wrapped around body, whiskers slightly back, ears slightly flattened, perhaps with one ear pointed in the direction the cat wants to take. This is the flight position in the fight-or-flight scenario, sending a message that the cat doesn't want a confrontation.

SITTING/RECLINING: Most often owners tell me this is when a behavior concern arises or happens seemingly out of the blue. A cat lying down, tail swishing and eyes dilated, is attempting to own the space. But if we have mastered the face and tail communication, incidents from these positions are less likely as clients are more aware of their cat's mood.

Actions

Your cat engages in different kinds of actions that can indicate various things. For example, when cats yawn and stretch, they might simply need to stretch their muscles and take in more oxygen. But yawning and stretching can also be a way for the cat to demonstrate they are confident around you. A nervous cat would never take such a risk.

HEAD BUTTING/FACE RUBBING: Properly known as head bunting, this is your cat's way of marking territory, saying, "This belongs to me." Consider it a special kind of compliment to be marked by your cat as their human. Cats who are friends can often be seen exchanging scents in this manner.

LICKING/GROOMING: Cats lick and groom each other when they are very comfortable together. They also lick themselves to feel better after a stressful incident as well as for general grooming.

FLEHMENING: All cats, even big cats, have a special organ in the roof of their mouth known as the vomeronasal organ. This sensory organ allows them to interpret scent and pheromones. A sniffing, slightly openmouthed, curled nose action indicates that your cat is learning something about the scent of you, another cat, or an object.

Playing/Hunting Behaviors

Cats are natural born predators, and activities like play or hunting are instinctual. As small predators, they have learned to take advantage of opportunity as well. Morning activity tends to arouse your cat, making them ready to hunt or play. You can find yourself the victim of an ankle attack from under the bed as your cat uses you as target practice.

One way to avoid this behavior is to use the "hunt, eat, sleep" method of modification. While you have your morning coffee, use a wand toy to play with your cat for 15 minutes, then feed the cat breakfast, which should trigger a sleep cycle.

WHAT ARE YOU SAYING TO YOUR CAT?

Cats are incredibly sensitive creatures of comfort. Many of the things your cat does or seeks to do are based on its needs. Learn what your cat thinks you are saying through your own behavior.

Earlier I mentioned that a person who ignores a cat is the one the cat will seek attention from. Ignoring the cat gives them time to assess the situation and determine whether the person is a threat. Rushing up to greet a cat is seen as an unwanted approach from which many cats will retreat.

Shouting at a cat or lots or loud activity in the home will cause a cat to become anxious.

Lights off at night when you are not home can be interpreted as abandonment. For that reason, our pet sitters turn on lights and play cat therapy music at night.

Ignoring your own cat can cause a deep depression. We think of cats as loners, but that is further from the truth than most people realize. When you consider their overall behavior, they display a deep desire to be with us.

Cats are masters of hiding physical discomfort. If you don't recognize the signs that your cat might be in pain, veterinary care might come too late to be effective or your cat might develop serious behavior issues.

You don't need to punish your cat. Cats do not receive punishment well and usually don't understand it. Yelling, spraying, kicking, or hitting your cat will only result in the cat feeling more fearful and anxious.

CHAPTER THREE

CAT RELATIONSHIPS

This chapter covers how cats relate to others—other cats, dogs, humans, and other animals.

Even though cats have lived alongside us for centuries, it is quite astonishing how little we know about their relationships and social structures. There is a big difference between what cats expect out of a relationship and what we think they are expecting.

CAT-CAT RELATIONSHIPS: AN OVERVIEW

The only thing solitary about cats is hunting. Contrary to popular myths, cats are very social animals, with a semi-fluid hierarchy. Depending on the resources available, the domestic house cat can often have successful cat-cat relationships, making it possible for several cats to live harmoniously within a single home.

However, we often make incorrect assumptions about our cats' social structures. Cats' social structures are not the same as ours, nor as those of dogs and other canine pack animals. If we consider cat hierarchy as a ladder, with each cat being on a different rung, we can understand the cat social structure more accurately. Each cat in the group can move up or down a rung or two, depending on the situation, the environment, and even who else may be in the room.

THE MULTI-CAT HOME

There are many benefits to having more than one cat if you have enough resources and the right environment to accommodate their instinctual needs. It allows them to be more "cat-like," with play, social interaction, and less destructiveness. An overcrowded environment with insufficient resources—such as cat trees, litter boxes, feeding stations, and drinking stations—can create territorial issues that result in behavior problems like fighting, spraying, and marking. Even in a very large home, there can be territorial issues and resource-guarding behavior if all the resources are too close together.

Introducing a New Cat

Bringing a new cat into your home is exciting, but many people make the mistake of rushing the introduction process. Let's start off on the right paw by looking at how you can introduce cats to your home with minimal problems. These steps are general guidelines. If hostility breaks out at any point, go back to the previous step.

WEEK 1: Set up a separate room for the new cat with everything they need. The cat will be in here alone for a week or more, so make them comfortable with food and water, a litter box, toys, a bed, and, if possible, a window so the cat can look outside. Include a night-light and a pheromone diffuser. There should be no contact with your other cat, not even by sight, although they will pick up one another's scent and may sniff around the door.

WEEK 2: If no serious growling and yowling has occurred after a week, open the door, set up a baby gate to keep the cats apart, and begin feedings and treats by the gate for both cats while you are there to supervise. Remove the gate after feeding and close the door. The cats will start to associate the new cat with good things happening. You can also begin swapping scents during the second week by swapping beds and blankets and perhaps brushing one cat and then the other cat. Continue with the treats and feedings at the baby gate. If you have more than one cat, depending on their reactions to their new housemate, this process can take place simul-taneously or separately for each cat.

WEEK 3: If things go well in week two, place your resident cat in a bedroom for the day, close the door, and let the newcomer out of their room to explore the house on their own. This gives the newcomer the chance to get oriented to the home without having to deal with a potentially hostile encounter. It also lets you observe the new cat and determine what resources interest them. At the end of the day, return the new cat to their room and let the resident cat out of the bedroom. Continue with the activities from week two.

WEEK 4: By this time, you should be able to allow both cats out into the home together. Typically the cats will have accepted each other, and a few days later the integration will be complete.

Keeping the Peace Between Cats

The most common reason I see for cats not getting along is a lack of resources: food, water, litter boxes, perching locations, sleeping areas, etc. In the multi-cat household, it is common for one or several cats to guard resources they perceive as valuable. Keep in mind that what you might think is valuable is often not what the cat thinks is valuable.

Litter box guarding is common. Cats like a clean box, and they like privacy. Dirty litter boxes and keeping them all in one location can trigger guarding. When a cat can't access the litter box, it will do its business somewhere else in the home. Make sure you have at least one more litter box than the number of cats and avoid crowding them in one area of the home.

Another resource that cats highly prize is territory. When I assess territory in a client's home, I look for perching locations, resting areas, pathways, windows, and vertical space. You can resolve territory issues by providing sufficient access to these areas or using cat trees to provide additional vertical space. A quick search of the Internet for modern cat furniture yields several designs that work both for cats and as human decor.

I have found that keeping the peace between cats is usually a matter of resources and territory. On rare occasions there can be an undiagnosed medical reason for problems, especially when a cat is not using the litter box. In those situations, you might need to consult your veterinarian.

SPECIAL CAT-TO-CAT CONSIDERATIONS

There are a few special circumstances to consider. One is introducing a kitten into a home with an older cat. I highly recommend assessing the older cat's health and temperament before bringing a kitten home. Older cats have their own set of special needs, and a kitten's high energy and rough play may be too demanding for the senior cat.

Stray cats in your yard can trigger a territorial reaction from your cat. This is especially true if the outside cats are using your garden beds as litter boxes or territorially marking around your house. Also, outdoor cat fights, even if your cat cannot see them, can make your cat feel anxious.

CAT-HUMAN RELATIONSHIPS

The cat-human relationship is spectacular. The domestic cat has gone from a mutually beneficial relationship of rodent control to pampered house cat in about 150 years. As of this writing, the domestic house cat is the most popular pet in the United States.

It is hard to say why humans love cats so much. I believe the reason may be that our relationship with cats is not based on appeasement behaviors as with dogs, but on what for so many centuries was an essentially separate but mutually beneficial relationship. We often talk to our cats, sharing our secrets with these enigmatic creatures as if they were human, and they respond to us with purrs, meows, and chirps. We bring food and provide the warmth of a mother cat when they snuggle with us. It has also been suggested that cats perceive us as just another really big cat.

Your Relationship with Your Cat

To improve your relationship with your cat, it helps to remember that it is one of mutual benefit. Learn your cat's sign language and not only its audible sounds. Being able to detect that your cat is anxious or in pain can go a long way in improving your relationship.

Enrich your cat's environment based on what interests them. That might be toys, interactive play with you, a birdfeeder outside their favorite window, or, believe it or not, cat-appropriate music. These resources help relieve the anxiety of boredom and keep them mentally fit.

Take the time to train and desensitize your cat to things that cause them fear, anxiety, or stress. Training your cat is in and of itself a great way to improve the bonds between you.

When looking for ways to improve your relationship with your cat, look for reliable resources and trained cat behavior professionals. The biggest mistake that many cat owners make is to follow advice that is based on unscientific information regarding cat behavior from poor Internet sources, social media cat groups, or reality

TV shows. You will find resources at the end of this book to help (see page 125).

Introducing Your Cat to a New Human

You and your cat have been together for a while. You have learned to understand each other. Now a new human being will be moving into the space that you and your cat have occupied alone. Your cat may not understand this new person in their life. You need to help get your new roommate or partner up to speed on cat basics and help your cat feel comfortable with the newcomer.

Start by introducing the new human's scent into the living space by leaving a worn sweatshirt, scarf, or even dirty socks in the home for a few days. Encourage the person not to run right up to greet the cat and not to be offended if the cat hides under the bed or somewhere else in the home the first few times they are around.

Let the cat determine if the newcomer is a friend or foe. Suggest that the new person sit on the floor with some treats and toss them in the cat's direction, then get up and walk away. Do not drag the cat out of their hiding place—the cat will determine when they feel safe enough to come out. By keeping things low-key, your cat is much more likely to welcome your new partner.

Cats and Kids

Many new parents are concerned about having a cat around a baby. Of course, you want to keep your baby safe from the cat. It helps to prepare the cat for the arrival of this tiny new creature. You can play recordings of the sounds a baby makes and let the cat explore the nursery. Keep in mind that baby items can seem like great cat toys and baby blankets can be inviting cat beds, so provide your cat with a desirable location in the nursery where they can observe the activities from a safe, comfortable perch.

If you already have young children when you bring a new cat into your home, teach your children how to treat the cat. Help them understand how to read a cat's body language and recognize signs of an angry cat. Never let your child wrestle with the cat using their hands or feet. Give the cat places in the home to get away from the children and retreat if the cat is feeling uncomfortable.

Most of all supervise, supervise, supervise! Accidents are bound to happen. Try not to get overly excited if a cat reacts to having its whiskers or tail inadvertently pulled too hard. The cat's reaction is normal, and it is up to you as the parent to teach your child that the cat doesn't like those kinds of actions. I have encountered parents who have literally flown off the handle, demanding that the cat be removed from the home, if their child gets scratched. I remind them that they need to find out what triggered the cat's reaction. Much like a child scraping a knee, these things are bound to happen.

CAT-DOG RELATIONSHIPS

We have all heard the phrase, "Fight like cats and dogs," but did you know that these two species can coexist? This unique relationship takes some time to develop and nurture, but it can happen. It's most likely to be successful when both animals are laid-back in nature and not given to a high level of anxiety. Fearful cats tend to run and hide, which can trigger the prey drive in even the best-trained dogs.

Introducing a Dog and a Cat

Bringing a cat into a home with a dog can be a challenge. Your dog should be well trained on basic commands before adding a cat into your home. Let's go over the steps for the best chance of success. If you are bringing a dog or puppy into your home with a cat, the roles here are essentially reversed. It is best if the adult dog has already been assessed to be cat-friendly. It is also helpful to know if your cat is dog-tolerant, too.

1. Give the cat a neutral dog-free space to decompress, the same way you would if you were going to introduce a new cat to a multi-cat home.

2. Use feeding time as training time for both animals. Start with feeding them both on either side of the closed door at distances that don't trigger a response.

3. If both animals are behaving well after a week, place a pet gate at the door for feeding. A pet gate is different than a standard baby gate. It has a small door along the bottom that is the right size for a cat to pass through but not big enough for a large dog or a toddler. At this point, the dog may be curious, and you may need to put distance between the two feeding stations. The proper distance is where both animals can eat without anxiety. Keep the pet gate door closed for now, and do not force the animals together.

4. After two weeks, place your dog in a separate room. Open the bottom door of the pet gate so the cat can explore the house without the dog around. This exploration helps the cat learn the layout of your home and find escape routes and hiding places if they should become frightened.

5. When both pets are eating calmly at the pet gate, you can begin face-to-face meet and greets. Put your dog on a leash and let the cat out of their room via the pet gate. It is important that your dog remain as calm as possible, so good dog training is essential. Use high-value treats to reward your dog for calm behavior. Let the cat come and go as they please. Repeat these sessions until you no longer see signs of stress or anxiety in either pet.

6. Next, keep the dog on a leash but allow it to drag loosely on the floor. Pay attention, and if the dog gets overly excited or starts to chase the cat, step on the leash to restrain the dog. Go back to step 4 or 5 and try again.

7. Continue to supervise meetings between the animals until there is no longer any tension between them.

8. When you are not at home, the pets should be kept separated until you are confident they have fully accepted each other.

Keeping the Peace Between Cats and Dogs

Once your cat and your dog are comfortable around one another, try to keep the relationship of these new buddies on an even keel. Giving food and treats while both are around is a great way to keep both animals thinking, "Good things happen when I see the cat/dog." Always make sure your cat has a place to go in order to get away from the dog.

Cats have a much longer memory than dogs. If things go wrong, the cat will take longer to feel safe around the dog, if ever again. Once predator-prey instincts are activated, they are very hard to undo, and the pets will need to be supervised much more closely in the future.

CATS AND OTHER ANIMALS

The general rule regarding cats and other animals is the larger the animal, the less likely they are to trigger the cat's predator and hunting instinct. Think about the barn cat that gets along with horses, pigs, cows, and even chickens yet works in the barn hunting mice and rodents. Conversely, the cat realizes all too well that they can also be the prey of animals like dogs, coyotes, owls, and larger wild cats. The duality of being predator and prey means the cat will likely hide from things that invoke fears at first encounters. The cat sets the tone and pace for learning, so you cannot force or rush the cat into new situations.

Certain types of pets may require extra precautions and extra supervision. For example, fish tanks may require a tank cover to protect the fish, rodents should be kept in protected cages, and birds should be placed in rooms with the door closed when no one is around to supervise.

The prey drive in a cat changes with age. A young cat is into hunting, but an older cat may not move unless there's significant activity to attract attention. Keeping in mind that every cat is different, interactions with prey-size animals are best conducted under direct supervision.

CAT CHRONICLES: BUSTER'S TERRITORY

Buster met me at the door hissing and growling. Buster had managed to chase off several cat sitters, and his owners could not have guests in their home unless Buster was locked safely away. Two other cats live in the house without issues and all three cats are littermates. All three cats are neutered male cats, and all are on a feeding schedule.

Buster's personality is such that he chooses to confront whatever he is afraid of. But the family lived in fear of him and had resorted to using squirt bottles and blockades. Once I had his full life story of feral kitten to house demon, my team developed a four-week plan for improvement.

We started with an assessment of the home environment. I thought it was important for the family to get Buster up off the floors as much as possible, with elevated routes around the main living room and dining room. But the step-down family room windows were at ground level, so when Buster jumped onto the cat tree in the family room, he wasn't up above things; in his mind he was still on the ground.

With no real way of fixing this problem, we suggested that the family rearrange the furniture so that the low windows would be unavailable or that they place privacy window films on these windows so the cats couldn't see out. We recommended using food puzzles and foraging stations on the elevated routes around the perimeter of the room they created for Buster.

When I returned for the three-week update and follow-up assessment it was clear Buster was much more pleasant to be around. His anxiety had been lowered to a tolerable level and he was no longer challenging people coming through the door to visit.

CHAPTER FOUR

PLAY AND HUNTING

As humans, we enjoy watching cats play, as evidenced by a quick browse through the abundance of cat videos online. Play is essential for keeping your cat happy and healthy, which affects its overall behavior. Play therapy is one of primary tools recommended and strongly encouraged to relieve a multitude of behavior problems stemming from stress, anxiety, boredom, and even fear.

THE PURPOSE OF PLAY

Our cats are natural born predators and opportunists. As they developed a mutually beneficial relationship with humans, we didn't need to teach them to kill the vermin around our food storage; we never needed to train them to do what they were born to do.

Playing, pouncing, and stalking are all common hunting behaviors, and it is a common belief that play is a form of hunting practice. Modern research, however, has found that for domestic cats, play behavior is less about hunting than it is about building the cat's long-term social structure. While we don't yet fully understand the differences between play and hunting for the cat, it is clear that play behaviors feature significantly in how well kittens develop socially with the world around them.

Play is also essential to the health of a cat's brain. It releases dopamine, which positively affects their overall behavior, and it helps the cat form a relationship with people, other cats, and other animals that might be in their environment.

TOYS

Every home should have at least five types of toys that cater to the cat's natural instincts for hunting.

FEATHER WAND: The feather wand, which is for supervised play, is by far a favorite for many cats. The feathers mimic a bird and, if the wand is long enough, the wand sounds like a bird in low flight. The drawback of this toy is that if left available to the cat when no one is around, they are likely to shred the feathers, just as they would do before eating a bird. Some feather wands also come with a fishing line. Be careful not to leave the wand where the cat could access it and become entangled in the line. Wand-type toys may also come with bugs, mylar ribbons, and more.

FOOD DISPENSING TOYS: There is a wide variety of food dispensing toys on the market these days. Their goal is to eliminate the unending bowl of kibble and to encourage your cat's natural hunting and foraging behaviors, helping to reduce stress and anxiety. You can find food balls with adjustable openings, like the mouse-shaped Doc & Phoebe's Indoor Hunting Feeder, that I recommend to my clients.

PUZZLE TOYS: Puzzle toys can be something like a busy box with multiple paw-sized holes for the cat to retrieve toy mice, bat a ball around, or even find a treat. It is important to start out with simple puzzle toys and work up to more difficult models so your cat does not become frustrated. The website Foodpuzzlesforcats.com has great examples of puzzles to buy or do-it-yourself ideas for making your own.

TOY MICE: These are my cats' favorites. They are just the right size for my cats to hunt. It's not unusual for my cats to drop them inside the front door while I am gone as a gift or to hear one of them proudly announce that they had caught (discovered) a new mouse. I keep a mason jar of toy mice mixed with dry catnip and rotate them weekly.

LASER TOY: There are opposing opinions on the use of the laser toy. If used too often, it can trigger light-neurotic behavior, as if your cat is chasing after every beam of light or reflection they notice. This behavior comes from a lack of closure to the hunting instinct because the cat never actually catches the red dot. In some cats, this frustration can result in redirected aggression or overgrooming. If you are going to use a laser, be sure that at the end of the dot session, your cat is able to catch a toy mouse or receive some food, so it feels the satisfaction of catching something.

HOMEMADE TOYS: Sometimes the simplest items are our cats' most favorite toys. Items like cardboard boxes to play and hide in, rustling packing paper or tissue paper to pounce on, and small items like bottle caps and milk rings to bat around or carry can delight your cat. I've met some cats that love to play fetch with these items. A caution: Avoid using aluminum foil balls, because the aluminum is toxic to cats if they decide to shred it or ingest it.

CATNIP

The herb *Nepeta cataria*, better known at catnip, has an intense behavioral effect on up to 70 percent of adult cats. Kittens don't seem to respond to it until sometime between the ages of three to six months. Responses appear to be genetic since there are cats that don't respond at all.

When cats sniff and roll around in catnip, they get excited. Cats that eat the herb experience a mild calming effect. The science is still out on what causes these reactions. Some researchers believe that the herb mimics a sexual pheromone, while others think it triggers "happy" receptors in the brain (although there are a few cats that become aggressive when exposed to it).

You can find dried catnip as well as fresh-growing catnip in pet stores or garden centers. Some cat owners have concerns about toxicity if their cats should eat plants in their homes. However, there are safe cat-friendly plants. Every summer I plant several containers of herbs for my cats to enjoy, including catnip, arugula, rosemary, parsley, and lemongrass.

SOLO PLAY

Curiosity and cats go hand in hand. Encourage your cat's curiosity by having them engage in solo play with puzzle toys and food dispensing toys, and by rotating fresh toys into their environment. Cats will stalk these new toys, pounce on them, and play with them.

Toys that cats like can be anything from toy mice to milk rings. I love to set up busy boxes for my cats. These are simple cardboard boxes with holes cut into them and toys inside. I like to use toy mice, treats, or catnip toys for the cats to find.

Cats become bored with solo play very quickly, so you need to rotate your cat's toys and place toys in novel locations for them to discover.

This might sound like a lot of work. But if your cat becomes bored enough, you can find yourself with the midnight "zoomies" or frantic runs through the house at full speed, usually at night when you're trying to sleep. The best way to avoid midnight zoomies is to understand the cat's cycle. Cats are most active during the evening and early morning hours. A good healthy play session before bedtime with a snack afterward can help set the sleep cycle in place. Providing the cat with food-dispensing toys to forage overnight can help eliminate early morning zoomies.

A word of caution here: If your cat does not normally display zoomies and begins to show hyperactivity, meowing, or yowling for no apparent reason, it is a good idea to get them checked out by your veterinarian. These can be symptoms of an underlying medical condition.

PLAYING WITH OTHER CATS

Kittens tend to play, learn, and practice hunting together. This play is part of learning a social structure. Kittens also engage in rough play with each other, during which you may notice their ears will be forward and claws will come out. They may even bite, but this is normal and shouldn't cause any damage. However, this type of play may get out of hand. If you notice a kitten with their ears back, hissing and growling, it's time to interrupt the play session—clap your hands loudly or use a pillow to separate the kittens.

Older cats can engage in rough play as well. When they're playing, the action will be reciprocal and there won't be any hissing or growling. Male cats will engage in rough play well into their adolescent years, while females will stop this kind of play by about two years of age. At that time, there can be a disruption in the social structure between a male and female cat. If this is the case, you can help manage the peace by using wand toys to burn off the male cat's play energy.

PLAYING WITH HUMANS

Playing with your cat provides exercise, mental stimulation, and an opportunity to bond. It helps to relieve stress, anxiety, boredom, and even in some cases aggression. Play-related communication with us should have your cat showing interest, with whiskers forward, ears perked up, and eyes slightly dilated. You can tell your cat needs more interactive play if you are noticing destructive behaviors, weight gain, aggressiveness, attention-seeking, or reclusive tendencies.

Play Time

A cat's interactive play occurs several times a day. I like to encourage a 10- to 15-minute morning and evening session, focused on the cat's natural activity cycles. I also recommend that the sessions end with a food reward. This does two things: it helps set the cat's natural hunt-eat-sleep cycle, and it signifies that good things happen when they interact with their human.

So what does interactive play look like? You should use wand-type toys and not your hands. Wand-type toys with feathers, ribbons, or mice on the end can be used to mimic prey: you are giving your cat a chance to "hunt" at home. You can be creative and set up craft paper, boxes, or tissue paper mounds that give your cat a chance to stalk the wand-type toy "prey" and pounce on

CAT CHRONICLES: MUDDY

One day, one of my clients brought home a beautiful young cat named Muddy from a shelter. Muddy proved to be extremely fearful. The only time she would come out from under the bed was for food, and any attempt to interact with her sent her running back to her hiding place. We set up some cameras to see what was happening during the day when no one was home. The cameras showed Muddy interacting with her environment normally and even playing with her toy mice and snuggling with the other cat. Yet the moment she heard the owner's car, she ran back under the bed.

We really wanted to build up Muddy's confidence and trust. I tried having the owner use a wand toy with a string attached and a mouse on the end, but this seemed to terrify Muddy even more. A laser pointer brought her out to the edge of the bed, but she was unwilling to engage beyond that.

Finally, we tried an inexpensive toy called a Cat Dancer, a simple wire with a few bits of cardboard rolled onto the ends. On the floor it sounds like a mouse scurrying around, and within moments it brought Muddy out from under the bed. Muddy's owner built up more trust with her with each play session by using this toy and keeping her own body movements small and controlled. Within a few weeks, playtime trust translated into Muddy enjoying the company of her human, knowing she wouldn't be harmed. She remained intensely fearful of wand- and stick-type toys all her life, but the Cat Dancer on a wire was her favorite toy to share with her owner.

it, hide it under crinkly paper, and dart from mound to mound. This is a wonderful chance to watch your little hunter in all their strength, cunning, and abilities.

Play Safety

Knowing how to play safely with your cat is important for you and for your children. Remember that during play, the toy is acting as prey for your cat. This means your cat will be using teeth and claws. Using a wand-type toy or a Cat Dancer (see page 45) helps you keep a bit of distance from your cat's hunting weapons.

Some cats can become overstimulated by play. This generally happens when they become frustrated by not being allowed to catch the toy. Be sure that you allow your cat to catch the toy, bite it, and mock kill it, even to drag it away so they can play with their prize catch. When a cat becomes overstimulated, you may need to toss the toy away from you, which will distract the cat from targeting you. If your cat is prone to aggressive play behavior, keep play sessions below their trigger threshold and end the play session with a serving of food.

HUNTING

For years it was believed that play was practice for hunting, but now we are learning that the two activities hold different purposes in a cat's world. One is a social and bonding activity, and the other is about getting better at foraging for food. Scientists are still exploring the role of play and how it is interpreted for hunting, as the behaviors are nearly identical. The purpose behind the context of these activities, however, is different.

Hunting, Indoors and Outdoors

Indoor play that simulates hunting and foraging gives your cat a very healthy, primal experience. But use caution when encouraging your cat to hunt live rodents that may invade your home. Mice, rats, and other rodents can carry fleas, diseases, and parasites; they might also have been poisoned by a neighbors' attempt to get rid of them. If your cat notices something scratching inside the walls, take alternative measures to rid your home of whatever is living in there.

Outdoor cats will naturally hunt wildlife, and there is little you can do to stop them. You can put a bell on the cat's collar to warn unwary birds and other prey. Another option is to not let your cat roam, but use a cat harness and leash when they are in your yard.

"Gift" Giving

One night my cat came up onto my bed but wouldn't settle down. I thought she was playing with the shadows on the covers. Frustrated, I turned on the bed lamp, and to my horror there was a tiny grey field mouse, barely alive, trying to get away from the cat.

You might wonder why your cat brings you dead or half-dead animals as gifts. In most cases it is your spayed female cat who is gifting you. She is hardwired to hunt and bring food back to her offspring. She wants to be sure you are well-fed or perhaps wants you to learn a few hunting techniques yourself! Give her a pat on the head, kind words, and a treat or meal. In the meantime, calmly remove the gory gift or frightened creature to safer lands.

CHAPTER FIVE

GROOMING

Cats groom themselves because they need to remove excess dirt, oils, food, or even scents from their bodies. Grooming is also thought to be a calming activity and a bonding behavior between cats and humans. Cats that consider each other friends will groom each other. Some cats will lick and groom their humans, too. This type of grooming behavior is called allogrooming and is only done amongst the closest of "friends."

CAT GROOMING BEHAVIOR

In between eating, sleeping, and hunting, a cat spends up to 50 percent of its time grooming. The cat's flexible body and rough tongue usually do this job very well. Kittens learn to groom themselves by two weeks of age and can perform the task on their own by the time they are ready to be weaned.

Cats groom for lots of reasons. Grooming helps distribute sebum, an oily, waxy substance, evenly throughout their fur, serving to coat and protect it. They groom after eating to remove food smells, the scent of the kill, from their fur so other predators won't be able to use that scent to hunt them. They groom themselves to clean up their back ends after using the litter box, and to calm themselves when they feel anxious or after a stressful event. Cats groom each other to share scent as a bonding and soothing activity.

Grooming is a natural behavior. If your cat stops grooming or begins to overgroom, you might need a trip to the veterinarian.

THE HUMAN'S ROLE IN GROOMING

Many people think their cat is self-cleaning, so they may never feel the need to groom or bathe their cat. But both short- and long-haired cats benefit from having grooming performed for them. Grooming your cat helps reduce hairballs and mats, giving you a chance to do a close inspection of the cat's coat and condition. A short-haired cat may only need human grooming once or twice a month, but a long-haired cat may need daily brush outs.

Introducing your cat to grooming is best accomplished when they are a kitten, although you won't have that luxury when you adopt an older cat from a shelter. Using the proper tools and being patient makes grooming part of the bonding process with your cat. Keeping it pleasant for both of you reduces stress and anxiety.

HOW TO GROOM YOUR CAT

When you groom your cat daily, they generally accept it as part of their relationship with you. Both of my cats enjoy our evening grooming sessions.

Daily grooming goes a long way with a long-haired cat to avoid a buildup of dirt and oils in their coat, helping keep the fur from becoming a tangled, knotted mat. When you encounter a mat in the coat, be careful not to pull it with your comb or brush, or your cat will begin to associate grooming with pain. Instead try to work it apart with your fingers, or try rubbing cornstarch into the mat itself and gently combing it out, starting at the ends furthest away from the skin. I have had a few mats take several days of gentle and patient combing to ultimately remove. Never use scissors to cut into a mat. A cat's skin is loose, and you can easily cause an injury.

Some people have electric grooming shears, and if you are comfortable using them, a quick shave of the spot will take care of a mat painlessly. Just be careful not to tug with the shears and cut into the skin.

If you are unable to remove the mat or your cat becomes unco-operative, stop grooming and schedule a visit with a cat groomer or your veterinarian. Also, if you have a long-haired cat, you might want to take a lesson from your local professional cat groomer.

ESSENTIAL TOOLS

» Cornstarch
» Flea comb (remove fleas, eggs, and dander)
» Greyhound comb
» Slicker brush with nubs
» Wide-tooth brush with nubs
» Wide-tooth comb

NICE TO HAVE TOOLS

» Furminator (helps remove loose fur)
» Grooming shears

CAT CHRONICLES: CHESTER

Chester was adopted as an adult cat. His long thick fur was matted from being confined in a kennel cage at the shelter. The shelter volunteers had tried to groom him, but his fractious response made it difficult and they were afraid of him.

Chester's adoptive owner, Shelly, contacted me looking for a referral to a groomer. Through our conversation, I learned that his original vet records stated he was normally fully sedated to be groomed.

I explained to Shelly that, if the records were accurate, she should speak with her veterinarian first before contacting a regular groomer. Thankfully she did, because Chester's vet detected a heart murmur. X-rays indicated that Chester was no longer a candidate for sedation and would need to be put on heart medication. Shelly was advised not to expose him to any stressful events for the next several weeks.

During these weeks, we worked to undo the damage done by Chester's previous grooming experiences. Understanding that grooming should be a positive social and bonding experience, we set about helping Chester gain trust with his owner. We used treats, gentle combing, and good kitty massages, and we ended grooming sessions while Chester was still purring. We did not try to cut or remove his mats; that would take a skilled groomer.

The weeks passed and Chester remained a calm and willing participant in the process of desensitization. Shelly paid attention to his body language and stopped grooming before he reacted negatively. Once Chester was cleared by his veterinarian, we set him up with a Master Cat Groomer. The groomer gave him a lion cut, because that gives both the cat and the owner a chance to start over without all the matting, pulling, and pain.

Today, Shelly can maintain Chester's fluffy fur, and she uses a pair of grooming shears to remove his mats if needed. Chester is much more agreeable to fluffing and primping without the need of sedation because his coat is properly cared for every day. Shelly reports that he now looks forward to their evening grooming sessions.

TOOTH AND NAIL

Brushing a cat can be easy enough, but taking care of their nails and teeth can be more challenging. This area of general cat care can have a significant effect on your cat's overall behavior and health. Here are a few tips to make it easier.

Dental

Cats are carnivores. Their teeth are designed to tear and shred their meals. Wild cats keep their teeth clean naturally because their overall diet includes bones and grass. For domestic cats, however, statistics indicate that 8 out of 10 cats have some sort of gum disease by the age of three mostly due to their diet. Vets used to recommend kibble because it was believed to mimic a wild cat's cleaning from bone crunching. We now know that the high level of carbohydrates in kibble contributes to the buildup of bacteria in the mouth, leading to dental problems.

Brushing your cat's teeth at least twice a week can have a significant positive impact on their overall health. Never use human toothpaste—the fluoride it contains is toxic to cats. Instead, use a toothpaste designed for cats and apply it with either a finger toothbrush or a piece of gauze. Cat Life Today did a survey of cat toothpastes and identified Virbac C.E.T. Enzymatic Toothpaste as their top pick. I like the enzymatic toothpastes as they only need to be wiped on the teeth to get the job done. You can also find water additives, treats from the vet, and assorted over-the-counter items to help keep your cat's teeth healthy in between brushings.

Nail Trimming

A cat's nails are retractable. If they get too long, they no longer retract and instead continue to grow, eventually curving into the paw pad. Your cat's nails should be trimmed approximately every two weeks, even if they have access to a scratch pad or post. Regular trimming keeps the nails and pads healthy. Consider using ergonomic clippers, which are easier to hold and have smoother action of the scissor blades themselves. Avoid nail clippers that actually crush the nail instead of providing a clean cut. If your nail clippers become dull, replace them.

Like us, cats have a "quick" in their nail, which is the seal that protects the nail bed. When you gently squeeze your cat's paw, the nail comes out and you can see this pink, blood-filled portion. If you trim too closely or cut into the quick, the nail will be painful and bleed. Keep a styptic pen or cornstarch handy to help stop the bleeding, just in case.

Most cats resist having their nails trimmed, which is why it's best to start your trimming routine when the cat is still very young. If you have an older cat, you will need to go through a desensitization process of gently handling the paw, rewarding with a treat, and working your way up to the actual trimming of the nail.

There is no shame in taking your cat to the vet or groomer to have their nails trimmed if your cat is noncompliant. Many vet offices will schedule and charge only a nominal fee for a "tech" visit at which your cat's nails will be trimmed. I recommend that you reward your cat with a treat immediately after or even during nail trims at the vet's office.

For more details on your cat's nails, see chapter 8 (page 83).

PROFESSIONAL GROOMERS

Locating a good cat groomer has many benefits for you and your cat. Both long- and short-haired cats can enjoy a day at the kitty spa if it is done right.

Consider a trip to the groomer if your cat has matted fur, kitty dandruff, or a greasy coat, or if there is some other issue you don't feel equipped to deal with. My own cat Atlas was prone to getting a greasy spot right above his tail area, commonly known as "stud tail." It would then mat up no matter how well I paid attention to the area. He had a visit with his Master Cat Groomer about every 8 to 10 weeks, and each time I could tell he actually felt much better for having seen her.

When looking for a groomer, consider the overall environment of the pet salon. Are there barking dogs? Is the groomer certified to groom cats? How does the groomer handle a fearful cat? There are several organizations that specifically certify groomers as Master Cat Groomers, who work only with cats and are trained in gentle handling techniques.

BATHING

Cats generally keep themselves clean on their own, but there might still be a time when you need to give your cat a bath. The cat might have spilled something on themselves or has diarrhea and needs help cleaning up their backside.

You will need several towels, several pitchers for water, and a cat shampoo. If your long-haired cat's fur is matted, remove the mats before bathing the cat. The water will only tighten the mat, making it more difficult to deal with. You might need to see a groomer if this is the case.

Tackling the bath doesn't need to be daunting. Start by placing a towel on the bottom of the bathtub, sink, or utility tub. The towel provides a firm footing for your cat. Fill several pitchers with warm water and set aside. Then fill the tub or sink with about two inches of lukewarm water and place your cat into the water.

Gently pour warm water from the pitcher over your cat. Using as little cat shampoo as possible, soap up your cat, avoiding the head area, then rinse the cat with more warm water from the pitchers. Once most of the soap is rinsed out, use the rest of the water for the final rinse.

Lift your cat out of the water, wrap them in dry towels, and dry them as thoroughly as possible. Do not use a blow-dryer because the heat from the dryer is too hot. Just let your cat air dry, and they will take care of any excess water in their coat.

GROOMING A SENIOR CAT

Cats over eight years old are considered senior cats. At about this age, they begin showing signs of mobility issues that may make self-grooming difficult, so they need your help. Your older cat will feel better if you care for their coat with daily, gentle grooming, brushing, and combing. While you groom the cat, stay alert for painful areas that might indicate arthritis and speak with your veterinarian regarding treatment options.

GROOMING ESSENTIALS

- [ ] Cornstarch
- [ ] Dental treats
- [ ] Enzymatic toothpaste
- [ ] Flea comb (removes fleas, eggs, and dander)
- [ ] Greyhound comb
- [ ] Nail clippers
- [ ] Slicker brush with nubs
- [ ] Soft bristle brush
- [ ] Styptic pen
- [ ] Wide-tooth brush with nubs
- [ ] Wide-tooth comb

NICE TO HAVE GROOMING TOOLS/ACCESSORIES

- [ ] Cat coat conditioner
- [ ] Cat grooming face brush
- [ ] Cat shampoo
- [ ] Dental water additives
- [ ] Ear wipes
- [ ] Furminator
- [ ] Grooming shears
- [ ] Grooming wipes
- [ ] Rubber grooming gloves
- [ ] Tear stain remover (for white-faced cats)
- [ ] Undercoat rake (essential for long-haired cats)

CHAPTER SIX

FOOD

Cats can be picky eaters. It is important to recognize when your cat is simply being picky about their food versus when they have an actual food aversion. Both of these situations can have devastating effects on the cat's physiology and metabolic balance.

A cat who is a picky eater can suffer from improper nutrition, leading to poor bone health and a weakened immune system. Improper nutrition can also contribute to lifelong cardiovascular issues resulting from a lack of the nutrient taurine. Many processed kibble and canned food products lose these nutrients as they are made; manufacturers then need to add it back in to meet AAFCO feed standards.

A cat that is refusing to eat is considered a potential medical emergency. A cat's liver is unable to process the cat's own fat stores quickly enough, which can lead to liver failure within as little as 24 hours. Always treat your cat's pickiness as a possibly serious issue.

HOW CATS THINK ABOUT FOOD

Your domestic cat is actually a skillful hunter and a working animal. Left to hunt on their own, the cat would eat several small meals a day, be physically active, and be mentally engaged with their environment. With a true carnivore instinct, the cat would be very likely to eat the prey they catch (mice, birds, and other small animals).

WHEN AND HOW MUCH TO FEED YOUR CAT

Modern domestic cats don't have much opportunity to hunt prey unless they live on a farm. Even feral urban street cats need a helping hand when it comes to food.

Our modern cat is often presented an overflowing bowl of dry kibble to eat at their leisure. This creates a host of problems, from pet owners not recognizing portion control to not realizing that their cat may not have eaten in days. There should be a chart on the food bag to help you estimate how much your cat should be eating of that particular food and help you know how often to fill the bowl. You might be surprised to find you are expecting your picky cat to eat too much or are providing way too much food.

Enter the automatic feeder. If properly set for portion control, it is a fine tool for feeding kibble. However, being smart hunters, cats can sometimes outsmart these feeders. Some cats do this by figuring out how to open the feeders.

Another problem is that feeders can create stress and anxiety as the cat waits for the next distribution of food. I often encourage a better alternative to these devices: food puzzles. Food puzzles engage the cat in their instinctive behaviors of working for their meals. They help reduce boredom and stress by enriching their entire world beyond the food bowl.

TYPES OF CAT FOOD

You are likely to have heard strong opinions about what foods are good and bad for cats. But it is important to keep in mind what might be right for one cat may not be right for another. Ultimately, what good is high-end boutique food if your cat doesn't like its smell, texture, or taste? I strongly suggest that you speak with your vet or veterinary nutritionist about what food would be best for your cat.

Wet Food

Because cats are carnivores, the true gold standard should be canned food served in mouse-sized portions. Canned food also provides the added water cats need to maintain proper kidney function.

There is a tremendous variety of canned food available. Most wet foods are lower in unneeded carbohydrates and higher in protein content. The downside of wet food is that you need to serve it on a schedule, so the food is delivered fresh. This can cause your cat a bit of food anxiety as they anticipate feeding time. One way to reduce their anxiety is to provide a brief play session (a "hunt") right before feeding.

Dry Food

I am sure you can tell by now that I am not a fan of dry food as the main meal for cats. But dry food does have its proper place in your cat's overall nutrition. Kibble stays fresh longer, can be left out for a cat to eat at leisure, and can replace high-calorie cat treats to reward the cat during training sessions. The drawback is that kibble is high in carbohydrates that the cat does not need. Along with the never-ending kibble bowl, unnecessary carbohydrates contribute to obesity. If you use kibble, be sure to follow the feeding instructions on the bag. Many of my clients are surprised to find that their cat should not be getting more than a half to three quarters of a cup of food per day.

Raw Food

Some owners may choose a raw diet because this is closer to the diet of a wild cat. But you will find that raw food is not recommended by the American Veterinary Medical Association because of possible cross contamination and risk of illness. Raw food also lacks specific nutrients your cat needs, so raw food manufacturers must add ingredients to make the food nutritionally complete and to meet nutritional standards.

There can be medical reasons for choosing a raw diet, however. I have had several veterinarians agree to a raw diet after all other methods to control a medical condition like chronic diarrhea have failed, or because a difficult-to-regulate diabetic cat does better on a diet devoid of excess carbohydrates. I encourage you to review the information about types of food at the Feline Nutrition Foundation website (feline-nutrition.org) and to discuss options with your cat's veterinarian if you want to feed a raw food diet.

Special Diets

Once in a while, your cat may need a special diet because of their age or medical condition. This can pose problems because some cats get hooked on certain foods and you can have a difficult time weaning your cat onto a special diet. To make it easier for your cat to transition to a new, medically necessary food, offer a variety of food options throughout your cat's life. You can also try different prescription foods if your vet recommends a special diet. Buy a small bag of the food and check to see you can get a refund if your cat won't eat it. I have found at times that my own cats may eat one brand of a prescription diet but not another brand.

KITTEN FOOD: Kitten food is high in calories and nutrients necessary for a growing cat. Depending on the breed of cat, your veterinarian can tell you when to transition to an adult food.

SPECIFIC BREED FORMULA: Certain breeds of cats, such as the Maine Coon and the Bengal cat, may need food designed for their particular genetic needs.

INDOOR CAT FORMULA: This food is generally supposed to be lower in calories and is for the adult indoor cat who is not very active.

SENIOR CAT FORMULA: This type of food, generally for cats over 10 years old, contains extra taurine, less fat, and slightly higher proteins to support the aging cat.

HAIRBALL FORMULAS: Generally available over the counter, this food has extra fiber to help move excess hair along the digestive tract.

RENAL SUPPORT FOOD: These prescription foods provide low to good quality protein and restricted phosphate content to slow damage to the cat's kidneys.

URINARY FORMULAS: These foods are designed to help prevent bladder stones or crystals from forming in the urine and may break down existing stones or crystals.

DIABETIC FORMULAS: These foods are designed to help manage feline diabetes.

HYDROLYZED PROTEIN FORMULAS: These prescription foods are for cats with certain sensitivities to dietary proteins.

CAT CHRONICLES: ICHABOD AND THE HOUSE OF PLENTY

It was a cold, rainy night when George noticed a pitiful gray cat taking shelter on his patio. He opened the door and offered the cat a plate of food. The cat ran over, growled over the food, and ate it. George noticed the cat was thin and the freezing rain wasn't about to stop, so once the visitor had finished eating, he carried the cat inside to a spare bedroom. By the next day, this cat daddy knew he had a new, somewhat emaciated cat.

Ichabod continued to growl over his plate of food, even striking out or swatting when George tried to fill the plate or pick it up after it was empty. They struggled together for a week. But as Ichabod began to feel better, gain weight, and realize that food was going to arrive consistently, the behavior subsided. George began introducing Ichabod to the other cats in his house, but he soon realized to his dismay that any food was a reason for Ichabod to fight. Ichabod would need to be fed separately from the other cats so he didn't feel that he needed to compete for what he perceived as a limited resource. George understood where this behavior came from, but he was not quite sure how to change it.

I encouraged George to use food puzzles and Doc & Phoebe's Indoor Hunting Feeder to help Ichabod learn that this new home was a place of plenty. We also used play and treat sessions to reduce anxiety levels with the other cats. Ichabod eventually relaxed about food when he realized there were plenty of resources available to him.

CAT TREATS

The role of treats in cat training is to reward the cat for performing a desired behavior. When you train your cat, use high-value treats, those you use only during training as opposed to any other kinds of treats you give your cat.

Types of Treats

HIGH VALUE: This is the food item that gets your cat's attention every time, which makes it best to use in training situations. High-value treats are typically boiled chicken, baby food, squeeze cheese, fish flakes, freeze-dried chicken or shrimp. Some manufacturers now offer small packets of pure chicken or even salmon fillets that you can use for training. These packets are not to be used to replace meals because they are typically not fully balanced or may be high in calories.

WET STICKS: Several manufacturers offer these as purees and mousse, perfectly sized for training sessions, easy to handle and deliver.

CAT TREATS: Typically, these are the treats you find in the pet store and give your cats whenever you want to. Some of these treats may rise to the level of high value.

HAIRBALL CAT TREATS: These treats contain extra fiber or oils to help with hairballs.

DENTAL TREATS: This treat is used as an adjunct for regular dental care.

PILL POCKETS: When you have to give your cat medication, you can hide the pill in one of these treats.

When and How to Treat

We often give our cats treats just because it is fun and helps us bond with them. Most manufacturers note on their packaging how many treats to give your cat per day. This guidance is important because treats are often high calorie and not nutritionally balanced.

Too many cat treats can be a culprit if your cat starts putting on weight, and they can lead to health complications if your cat is on a prescription diet.

During a training program or behavior modification program we may ask you to limit the number or types of treats you give your cat and to use them only for rewarding the behaviors we want to reinforce. Providing similar treats outside your training times will dilute the value of the reward and make training more difficult. So keep those high-value treats set aside for training.

HUMAN FOOD

In the behavior modification and training world, we often use human foods to elicit a desired behavior. We may use tiny cubes of chicken or cheese, meat baby food, or even a squeeze cheese. These foods are used as high-value rewards for behaviors we need the cat to perform. They are used only in short sessions and never given as substitute meals.

Giving human-type foods as meals or substitute meals can trigger your cat to begin to snub regular cat food. Giving your cat morsels of food while you are cooking or at the dinner table can reinforce begging or even food aggression, and it's a nutritionally unsound practice. Getting human food as meals can make it hard for your cats to return to normal cat food. It can set the cat up for food aggression, food guarding, and begging. Reinforcing unwanted behavior with a high-value reward is also unwise and unfair to the cat. Training your cat out of these unwanted behaviors will be difficult and will require tremendous patience.

POISONOUS TO CATS

There are several common food items, medicines, and plants that are poisonous to cats or can cause them gastrointestinal upset. Please avoid them or keep them out of your cat's reach. Below are a few of the most common items. For a more extensive list, check the ASPCA website at aspca.org/pet-care/animal-poison -control. If your cat accidentally ingests any of these items, seek prompt medical assistance.

» Common pain relievers like aspirin, Aleve, Advil, and MOTRIN will kill your cat, so seek out an emergency vet.
» Anything containing xylitol, the substitute sugar found in many food items, is poisonous to cats.
» Plants in the lily family, including lilies, onions, and garlic, are highly toxic to cats. Even licking the pollen from a lily off their fur can cause death.
» Chrysanthemums, daisies, tulips, hyacinths, and daffodils are poisonous to cats.
» Marijuana *(cannabis sativa)*, which is currently legalized in many states, is also poisonous to cats.

WATER

Cats often do not get enough water. Your cat should be getting about a cup of water per day, depending on their weight. The formula is three to five ounces of water per five pounds of body weight; a 12-pound cat should be drinking a little over a cup a day.

A strictly kibble diet often leaves a cat in a state of minor dehydration. In order to be sure your cat is getting enough water, you can add a little extra water to their canned food and provide several watering bowls around the home. Many cats enjoy a cat water fountain. The moving water encourages them to drink more. Watch for a sudden increase in a cat's water consumption as it could indicate a medical condition needing *prompt* attention.

PICKY EATERS

It is said that cats are picky eaters, and to a large extent they can appear that way to their owners. Through research we are learning that a cat's pickiness about food is more genetically related to their evolution than first believed. Surprisingly, according to the Waltham Petcare Science Institute, cats can distinguish the nutritional value of their food, and when given a choice they will gravitate more toward a food that has a 50:50 ratio of protein to fat. As of yet, researchers don't know how cats can make this distinction between foods, but that doesn't mean we can't use that information with the picky eater.

Variety

Research from Waltham indicates that cats first go to a food based on the aroma. When the same foods were introduced over a course of time, eventually the cats settled on the food that most closely mimicked the protein/fat/carbohydrate content they would get from hunting prey. To expand your cat's palate, start by introducing a wide variety of flavors, aromas, and textures to your picky eater.

Give your cat several choices over the course of a few weeks and see which food they prefer.

Bowls

Consider the type of bowl or plate you are using to feed your cat. Deep, high-sided bowls have been shown to cause something called "whisker stress." Whisker stress happens when the cat has to place their muzzle into a too-small space to obtain food. Flat plates and low-sided bowls can potentially help relieve this issue. Also, some cats may not like a plastic bowl. Plastic can be a cause of chin acne in cats.

Portion Control

Picky eaters can be letting you know that their overflowing bowl of kibble has gone stale, rancid, or moldy. It is also possible you may be giving your cat too much food so your cat is simply not hungry. Check the package for feeding portions. I have had more than one client suddenly realize the portions recommended were for daily feeding, not per meal.

Reading Labels

In all honesty, figuring out cat food labels can take a doctorate level degree (just kidding).

Interpreting the labels gets particularly confusing due to the way some of the terms are used. A food label that says "chicken cat food" must contain at least 95 percent chicken. But a cat food that says "chicken with any other ingredients" might only contain 3 percent chicken. A product label that uses words like "chicken dinner," "chicken entrée," or "chicken platter" can have a range of 25 to 95 percent chicken, so you would need to take a close look at the guaranteed analysis to see what the protein-fat ratio really is. If your picky eater turns up their nose, they might be telling you that the food you're offering isn't quite up to standard.

Here are the basics to look for:

INGREDIENTS: By law, the label must list the ingredients in order of highest to lowest by weight. This means that the ingredients listed first contain the most moisture because moisture adds weight. On a kibble formula, this means that the first ingredient listed, say chicken, was weighed before being dehydrated.

GUARANTEED ANALYSIS: This describes the amount of protein, fat, and fiber in the food. Read the analysis to determine how close to the 50:50 ratio of protein to fat the food actually is.

FEEDING DIRECTIONS: These are the manufacturer recommendations for how much of their food to feed your cat. Keep in mind that your cat may need more or less depending on their current body condition and activity level.

NUTRITIONAL ADEQUACY STATEMENT: This statement tells you what life stage of the cat—or in some cases, the breed—the food is for, such as kitten, adult, senior, Bengal, or Maine Coon.

OVERWEIGHT CATS

Carolyn McDaniel, VMD and lecturer at Cornell University's College of Veterinary Medicine, says about 50 percent of the cats they see are overweight to obese. Purina and Hill's both provide free body scoring charts to help you determine your cat's ideal body conformation; if you cannot feel your cat's ribs under a layer of fat, then your cat is obese. Much like humans, cats who are overweight or obese can suffer from major medical diseases like diabetes, arthritis in the back and joints, and strain to the cardiovascular system.

The most likely cause of a cat being overweight is "free feeding," the unending bowl of kibble that over half our cats enjoy every day. The anecdotal evidence is clear in the feline overweight epidemic: cats don't successfully self-regulate their food intake. Ideally, you should feed your cats canned food with a higher protein and moisture content. If you use a dry food, give it in the amounts recommended on the bag and provide it as part of a food foraging program or scheduled meals.

Before putting your cat on a diet, consult your veterinarian. Cats have specific needs to consider for a weight reduction program because their livers do not metabolize fat very well. If you try to reduce the cat's weight too quickly, they can end up with fatty liver syndrome, which can be life-threatening.

CHAPTER SEVEN

THE LITTER BOX

One of the most common problems cat owners face is a cat who won't use the litter box. This chapter will help you understand how cats think about the litter box so you can make sure they use it in a healthy way. While every cat is different when it comes to litter box habits, here are some basics to consider.

CAT ELIMINATION INSTINCTS

Cats have a natural instinct to use an acceptable substrate that lets them dig and bury their urine and waste. In the wild, cats seek out secluded areas in which to eliminate so as not to attract predators. The same instinct drives our house cats to a quiet place in the home where they can do their business away from loud machines like washers and dryers or even other cats.

Normal elimination behaviors shouldn't be confused with territory marking or what is commonly known as spraying. Male cats are notorious for spraying, but female cats can do this as well if there are too many stressors in the home. Spraying behaviors have significantly different reasons and require different behavior modification strategies.

LITTER BOX BASICS

Cats can be fussy about their litter boxes. All cats prefer a clean litter box. Scoop them at least once a day and give them a more thorough cleaning at least once every two weeks, if not every week. Use plain soap and water. Ammonia cleaners will only enhance urine odors, and many litter boxes are antibacterial, so a simple cleaning is enough. In the summer or in warmer climates, I like to set the boxes out to dry in the sun because the UV light also decontaminates the box.

The general rule is that you should have one box more than the number of cats. As far as the cat is concerned, boxes placed side by side are one big box, so when setting up multiple boxes it is important to not place them all in one location. If you don't have the space, you'll need to scoop more than once a day. By placing the boxes in various locations, you reduce the chance of litter box guarding, which creates anxiety for some cats.

THE BOX

Choosing the right size litter box for your cat is important. Most cats need a box that is about one and a half times bigger than they are.

KITTEN LITTER BOX: The small litter boxes you may see in the pet store are designed to help the kitten have easy access both into and out of the box.

STANDARD LITTER BOX: This is the litter box for cats that weigh about 10 pounds.

LARGE LITTER BOX: Cats over 10 pounds need this larger litter box.

HIGH-SIDED LITTER BOX: These boxes are designed for cats that either don't squat when they urinate or start to stand up before they are finished. They are great for cats that tend to urinate over the edge of the box.

HOODED LITTER BOX: Some cats prefer a hooded box, while other cats hate them because they feel too small and allow for ambushing at the box. These boxes usually have a carbon filter in the top to help control odors; owners like the hoods, which helps control litter scatter.

AUTOMATIC LITTER BOX: These fancy boxes are designed more for the owner than the cat. They are filled with crystal litter that traps urine and odors while a grate automatically scoops clumps or feces into a compartment for later disposal. The biggest issue with this type of box is owners sometimes neglect to monitor their cat's litter box habits and can miss medical conditions that can lead to the cat not using the box at all.

HOMEMADE LITTER BOX: Owners often use their own storage boxes to provide a litter box that is large enough to prevent the cat from peeing over the edge. Storage bins are typically used as home-made litter boxes, and they are often less expensive than your average litter box.

TOILET TRAINING

In all my years I have only met one cat out of thousands that was toilet trained. The cat maintained an entire bathroom to himself. The owner used double-sided tape around sinks, etc. to prevent the cat from using them to eliminate instead of the toilet. Without the cat's instinctual need to dig and bury in a substrate, everything in this particular bathroom appeared as a toilet to the cat. Although toilet training your cat may seem like a huge benefit to you, ultimately if your cat should need to use a litter box at the vet or groomer, it may become an issue. Also, as your cat ages, they may not be able to safely jump up to the toilet seat and instead will choose to eliminate somewhere else. If that happens, you may have a hard time getting them to use a litter box.

THE LITTER

Choosing the substrate or litter that your cat will use can be a daunting task. Every year there seems to be something new on the market. Let's look at all these options with one thing in mind: "What does my cat prefer?" One note: I recommend staying away from artificially scented litters. When given a choice, cats almost always choose an unscented litter.

CLUMPING CLAY LITTER: Made from bentonite, which is an absorbent form of clay, clumping clay litter makes it easier to keep the litter box clean. If you scoop every day, the litter can last up to two weeks.

BASIC CLAY LITTER: This is the old-fashioned clay litter we used years ago, and it does not clump. While it does absorb urine, scooping it daily can be difficult as you will invariably leave some urine-soaked clay in the box, which causes odors. You will need to change the litter frequently because when your cat smells the odors, they might think the box isn't clean.

SILICA GEL CRYSTALS: Similar to gel beads such as moisture-controlling desiccants, silica gel crystals are highly absorbent, control odor very well, and are pretty much dust-free. They have their downsides. Cats can get the crystals stuck in their paws or even eat them, which is not healthy.

RECYCLED PAPER: This is paper that has been turned into pellets. The pellets are dust-free, absorbent, and biodegradable. The drawback is that they do not form clumps, which makes it difficult to scoop the litter box daily. You will end up changing the litter more often so that odors don't make your cat think that the box isn't clean.

PINE: Pine litter is treated to remove toxins that are harmful to the cat. It usually comes in the form of pellets that degrade to sawdust and is biodegradable. This type of litter is not scoopable.

WALNUT SHELLS: Crushed walnut shells have clumping ability and good odor control. They are also biodegradable.

ACCESSORIES

In addition to choosing the right litter for your cat's litter box, you will need a number of accessories.

LITTER SCOOPS: When looking for a litter scoop, be sure it is sturdy enough to not break easily with use and is appropriate for the type of litter you are using.

LITTER BOX LINERS: Most cats do not like liners in the box. They can snag their claws in them. Once that happens, you will have urine accumulate under the liner and create odor.

LITTER MATS: Litter mats are fine as long as the cat will walk on them. Again, this is a matter of the cat's preference, so you may need to experiment. I like to use a washable cotton braided rug instead.

ODOR CONTROL ITEMS: Nature's Miracle is an enzyme cleaner that breaks down urine salts. White vinegar on fresh urine will also break down the urine salts and eliminate odor. Cat Odor-Off by Thornell uses a proprietary blend of essential oils to bind up urine odors and can be used with other cleaners.

CAT CHRONICLES: TIG

Tig's owner, Julie, was getting ready to sell the house, and there was a lot of activity. All three of Julie's cats were becoming anxious as painting and repairs progressed.

When rooms were staged, the realtor told Julie to relocate the litter boxes to the basement laundry area. Shortly after the litter boxes were moved, Tig began urinating on the carpeting behind the sofa. Julie reached out to me immediately.

I quickly realized that putting all four litter boxes together in the basement set the cats up for a litter box guarding situation. One cat started hanging out under the steps and pouncing on anyone coming down the steps or into the laundry room. Tig, being a shy cat, had become terrified to go to the basement or would go down only when Julie took laundry downstairs.

To resolve this issue, I suggested that Julie put one box in an upstairs bedroom. Once Tig realized he had a box of his own again, he stopped urinating behind the sofa. Julie treated the area with Nature's Miracle and then followed with a spot steam clean with Cat Odor-Off.

HELP! MY CAT WON'T USE THE LITTER BOX!

Cats don't stop using the litter box because they are angry with you or feeling upset because of something you have done. When your cat quits using the litter box, your first step is to have the cat checked by your veterinarian to see whether there is a medical or environmental reason for the change in behavior.

SEEK MEDICAL HELP: More often than not, cats leave their litter box because of a medical issue. Urinary tract infections and stones or crystals in the bladder make for painful urination, which will chase a cat out of the box faster than anything else. Even constipation can lead to your cat leaving the litter box in pain. It might take several trips to the vet to find the appropriate treatment or to eliminate medical problems as the reason for your cat leaving the box.

CHANGE THE LITTER BOX: After any underlying medical condition has been treated, changing litter boxes might help get the cat back to using the box. The old box and its scent may be telling your cat that it is the place of pain and discomfort. A new box sends a signal that this will be different.

USE A DIFFERENT TYPE OF LITTER: Changing the substrate used in the box provides a different scent and texture that can encourage your cat to use the litter box again. I find Dr. Elsey's Cat Attract Litter helpful because it has an attractant and is soft on the paws.

ADD MORE BOXES: You can try putting out some additional boxes near where your cat has been eliminating. I often recommend doing this with several types of litter and letting your cat choose. Leave the boxes out for a week or two, until you can decide what's working.

PUT MORE BOXES IN DIFFERENT PLACES: This solution helps if you have multiple cats and one of them is litter box guarding. Giving each cat a different place to eliminate without being ambushed generally resolves the problem.

KEEP THE LITTER BOX CLEAN: Keeping the litter box as pristine as possible really does encourage your cat to use it.

TRY A GRADUAL RETURN: You might need to try this if your cat refuses to go anywhere near a regular litter box. Start out with a cookie sheet or boot tray and the cat's current chosen substrate—we've tried carpet, potting soil, shredded newspaper, play sand, and puppy pads. Over the course of several weeks, work your way back to using regular litter in a regular litter box. Having a complete history and working with your veterinarian or cat behaviorist can really help.

ADDRESS ANXIETY: If your cat is suffering from a generalized anxiety, your veterinarian can recommend actions or perhaps prescribe drugs to help with the behavior modification process.

CHOOSE FINER OR SOFTER LITTER FOR A DECLAWED CAT: Cats that are declawed are far more sensitive in their paws and feel pain much earlier than a cat who is not declawed. For that reason, they may avoid boxes with litter that is rough, sharp, or pointy. Choosing a finer grain or softer litter can help you avoid this issue.

CHAPTER EIGHT

SCRATCHING

There is nothing worse than walking into your home and seeing your cat scratching away on your sofa, carpet, or worse, the antique chair in the corner. Destructive scratching is a common problem most cat owners face at some point. Let's look at why cats scratch and what you can do about it.

WHY CATS SCRATCH

There is little difference between wild cats and the domestic cat regarding the scratching behavior. Scratching is actually a necessary function in the cat's world for both physical and mental well-being.

Cats scratch to help shed the outer layer of their claws, keeping them sharp. They scratch to get a good long stretch and loosen the spine. They scratch to mark territory by leaving subtle scent markers from their pads behind, and they scratch to leave visual markers on objects in their territory. Not being able to scratch can cause serious problems with the cat's nails and can create anxiety.

DON'T DECLAW

Cats are declawed by amputating the third phalange and claw. This controversial procedure is banned in several European countries, and several states in the United States are moving to do the same because declawing is increasingly understood as a serious injury to the cat.

The current belief is that declawed cats are more prone to higher anxiety, chronic pain in the paw and radial nerves, and back pain resulting in higher stress levels. These complications result in long-term behavioral changes, including urination outside the litter box, litter box aversion, chronic anxiety, and higher fear responses.

However, experts still do not completely agree about the effects of declawing. In July 2019, the American Veterinary Medical Association (AVMA) conducted a review of all the scientific literature and concluded, "There is conflicting scientific evidence about the implications of declawing." The veterinary community remains conflicted, with about 50 percent of veterinarians being opposed to the procedure. Still, the AVMA encourages owners to try other options before having their cat declawed.

One alternative to declawing is to use nail covers or caps. These can be applied at your vet office, by your groomer, or at home. They are applied with an adhesive and need to be changed every four to six weeks like a manicure. Some cats resist having nail caps and require sedation to apply them, so this is not a lasting solution for destructive scratching. It is far better to learn to trim your cat's nails and redirect them to appropriate scratching surfaces.

HELP! MY CAT WON'T USE THE SCRATCHING POST!

Humans often think that cats scratch their furniture to act out or call attention to themselves, but usually the cat is only doing something they need to do in a way that feels best. Let's look at a few ways to give your cat the scratching exercise they need and to redirect them away from your furniture, carpet, and other surfaces.

Surface Type

Consider the surface your cat is currently scratching. Certain types of upholstery are notoriously attractive to cats. These are nubby textiles and linens that the cats can dig their claws into. When replacing furniture, consider something with a much tighter weave to discourage scratching.

Not ready to replace furniture just yet? It's time to employ some serious distraction and deterrents. One of my first recommendations is to cover the desired scratching area with a double-sided tape called Sticky Paws. This tape covers the visual and scent markers, and cats don't like the way it feels. If Sticky Paws doesn't work, you can try a tight-fitting sofa cover or a plastic furniture protector.

Another way to deflect the cat from ruining your furniture and carpets is to place a scratching post in the same location as the object being scratched. Spray the post with catnip and use a knife to disturb the fiber on the post, creating both a visual marker and scent marker to the cat. After the cat has started using the post, you can slowly relocate it to another place in the room.

CAT CHRONICLES: MIKEY

Mikey had decided the area behind the bedroom door was a great place to start scratching up the looped-weave carpet. He had lived in this apartment for several years, but this was a new behavior.

I toured the luxury apartment with Alice, Mikey's owner, noting several well-used sisal rope pads on the floor and another hanging untouched on the doorknob to the bedroom. After discussing Mikey's scratching habits, we decided to try several more options.

As I pulled out a cardboard scratcher with a wave shape, Mikey immediately responded. I didn't even need to add catnip to it. Mikey proceeded to use the board very vigorously for several minutes, scratching, walking away and then coming back to it as if to tell us, "This is what I needed!"

Alice somewhat sheepishly admitted she had forgotten how much Mikey loved those cardboard scratch pads. We asked building maintenance to repair the damaged carpet behind the door and we used the Feliway spray to help deter any further damage. Mikey had a pawdicure and Alice soon replaced the small cardboard scratcher with a large wave-shaped cardboard lounger for him to relax on and scratch away to his heart's content.

Scratching Posts

When choosing a scratching post, consider the size of your cat. If your cat is large, your scratching posts needs to be of sufficient height or length for the cat to enjoy it. If the post is too small or made of the wrong material, your cat will not use it.

Not all scratching posts are vertical; in fact, some cats prefer a horizontal surface. If your cat likes to use your looped nubby carpet as a scratch pad, give them a cardboard scratch pad as an alternative. Then repair or cover the damaged area of carpet so it doesn't continue to attract the cat. Keep in mind that simply covering the damage with a large plant or a piece of furniture will only make the cat look elsewhere, so be sure they have another good option first.

Stability

The stability of the scratch post or pad is critical. If the pad or posts are unstable or flimsy, your cat is unlikely to use it after one or two attempts. Scratching behavior is a vigorous activity and if the pad or post moves or tips, it is not going to get the job done.

Feliway

Feliway is a popular pheromone product used for modifying multiple behaviors, from urine marking to destructive scratching. When using this product for destructive scratching, spray the surface you want your cat to *stop* using, not the one you want the cat to use.

Cat Trees

Cat trees often offer several scratching areas at several different angles. Encourage your cat to use these areas by rubbing a little catnip on them or spray them with Feliscratch.

Sisal Rope Pads

I see these from time to time in client homes. They are usually designed to hang from a doorknob to stop destructive scratching on doorframes or baseboards. But this type of scratching is territorial marking, so we often need to assess the home further and make bigger adjustments to alleviate the situation. In any event, hanging a sisal pad from the doorknob fails the stability requirements of a cat that needs to scratch out their territory.

CHAPTER NINE

SOLVING COMMON PROBLEMS

his chapter discusses solutions to common cat behavior problems. As you've already seen, those problems can have a variety of causes, from undiagnosed medical conditions to an environment that doesn't meet the cat's needs. Every cat is different, and there are many different factors that influence an undesired behavior, so it can take time and patience to determine what is really going on. It can also take several weeks to several months to resolve the problem—quick fixes are rare.

AN OVERVIEW OF BEHAVIOR MODIFICATION

When we're working with cats, we define behavior modification as the extinction of unwanted behaviors using learning techniques, desensitization, counterconditioning, and shaping. We avoid using negative techniques or flooding techniques (forcing a cat to experience negative stimuli) as they can make the cat worse and trigger other negative behaviors by increasing fear and anxiety.

Behavior modification starts with first determining if the cat has any health, nutritional, or physical factors that might be causing the behavior. I tell new clients we cannot change behavior if we are dealing with a medical issue, so we ask them to take the cat to their vet before we start working with them. I also ask for an extensive history of the cat or cats in the home. The history can give us good clues to the reasons behind the undesired behavior or why previous attempts at behavior modification may have failed.

Next, we will assess the cat's environment and work with you to identify changes to make. This might include rearranging furniture, adding cat trees, and looking for trigger situations that can be changed. The purpose of these first two phases is to reduce or remove any stressors that might be causing the problem behavior.

Once the first two phases are in place, we begin to provide positive reinforcement of the desired behavior and remove any existing rewards for the behavior we don't want. We may also provide passive deterrents to unwanted behavior, such as Sticky Paws, pheromone sprays, or air cans.

As the cat's behavior continues to improve, we start to remove the passive deterrents. This helps to reinforce the desired behavior. There will be some successes and failures as the cat continues to learn the new behavior, but eventually we reach a point where the new behavior becomes permanent and the old behavior is what we call extinct.

AGGRESSION

Cat aggression can strike fear into the heart of anyone who has ever been the recipient of an attack from a cat. Cat bites can cause serious infections that require hospitalization. According to the Cornell Feline Health Center, "A recent study reported that 27 percent of cats relinquished to shelters for behavioral reasons were surrendered for aggression." By recognizing your cat's body language and understanding that almost all aggression comes from a place of fear or discomfort, you can untangle the triggers and find solutions to the behavior. Generally, most aggression cases can be resolved in four to six months, typically with the help of your veterinarian and/or cat behavior consultant.

Note: Aggression that cannot be managed by what is covered in this book may require the help of a certified cat consultant or veterinary behaviorist. A veterinary behaviorist is a separate specialty of veterinary level medicine above the level of a regular vet, cat consultant, or a cat behaviorist.

Food-Related Aggression

In a multi-cat household, food aggression is often related to a perceived lack of resources. The cat might have been starved at some point in their life, or they might have a disease like diabetes, hyperthyroidism, or chronic kidney failure. Once a medical issue has been ruled out, we introduce the cat to what I call the House of Plenty.

» Using appropriate food portioning, we start feeding the cat separately.
» Using a baby gate, we start feeding the cats near each other until no aggression is shown.
» We introduce food puzzles and food foraging toys/games that help to mimic the hunting of food.
» We use the hunt, eat, sleep program so the aggressive cat works out their anxiety and then is rewarded with food.
» We set up feeding stations around the house that change location daily, paying attention to food proportioning.

If the cat is aggressive or begging for human food, we train them to have a certain place to go for food, eventually having them sit in a certain spot as meals are eaten. This training activity takes time, and I will cover the technique in chapter 10 (page 109).

Petting Aggression

Petting aggression is when the cat is purring and seems happy and relaxed while sitting on your lap but then suddenly starts biting or scratching at you. This is the result of overstimulation.

Limit petting to the area around the head and neck. Do not use big long strokes along the cat's body. Pay attention to your cat's body language while you're petting. If you notice flattened ears, tail twitching, or tensing up, or if the cat stops purring or even begins a low growl, stop petting, stand up, and let the cat jump to the floor on their own. The cat needs to calm down, which could take a few seconds to several minutes.

The sudden development of petting aggression when a cat hasn't shown it in the past might indicate that the cat is feeling pain or discomfort, anything from arthritis to dental disease or just not feeling well. It is best to take a trip to the vet to see what might be going on.

Handling Aggression

Cats with handling aggression don't like to be picked up or restrained. In fact, most cats don't like to be restrained at all, and forcing the issue can lead to an aggressive reaction. When picking up a cat, you want them to feel secure. Watching for dilated eyes, flat ears, or a swishing tail can go a long way toward avoiding an incident.

To desensitize a cat to being handled:

1. Place your hands on the sides of the cat, but do not lift. Release your hands and reward the cat with a high-value treat. Repeat five to ten times a day for a week.
2. When your cat has become comfortable with this amount of handling, place your hands on their sides and lift them several inches off the floor. Hold the cat for several seconds, then

reward them with a high-value treat. As your cat relaxes into the process over the course of a week, gradually increase the holding time.

3. Finally, try lifting your cat and holding them for several seconds. Release your cat before they start to struggle and give them a reward. Gradually increase the length of time until your cat becomes comfortable being held.

Redirected Aggression

Redirected aggression occurs when the cat is overstimulated by something they observe, such as another cat, a dog, a squirrel, a bird, or even a person. If your cat is exhibiting signs of redirected aggression at a particular window, I suggest blocking the view to the outside with window film. If the aggression is triggered by loud people in the home startling or scaring the cat, try to reduce the human behaviors; for example, teach children to use their inside voices.

In cases of redirected aggression, it is best to separate the cat from the trigger so they can calm down. One way to do that is to cover the cat with a large towel or an overturned laundry basket and shuttle them to a safe area. It can take several hours for the cat to calm down.

Territorial Aggression

As I said earlier, territorial inter-cat aggression is often the result of insufficient access to resources. Cats displaying this aggression need to be separated for several weeks and gradually reintroduced after you've created additional resources such as feeding stations, litter boxes, and vertical space.

One behavioral symptom of territorial aggression/anxiety is urine spraying and marking. Your cat is trying to communicate their anxiety by staking out territory.

If territorial cats can smell the marked area, they will return to it over and over again. You can use a black light to locate the marked areas and treat them with an enzymatic cleaner. If one cat is marking, it is also not unusual for a second cat in the house to be marking, too. In order to determine who is doing the deed, try separating the cats for a few days. If that doesn't work, you can add a food-safe fluorescent dye to their food, one cat at a time, to help determine which cat or cats are spraying or marking.

The measures to lessen this kind of aggression in cats often benefit from the use of antianxiety medication during the behavior modification process. Ask your veterinarian for a recommendation.

To deal with territorial aggression:

» Thoroughly clean all sprayed/marked areas and use a Feliway diffuser in those areas.
» Use interactive play and feeding stations in previously soiled areas.
» Cover windows or restrict access to places where the cat can observe other animals or people outside the home if these are triggers for the behavior.
» Immediately put away any new items brought into the home.
» To help relieve high levels of anxiety, provide the cat with more environmental enrichment through twice daily play sessions.

Fear Aggression

Fear aggression is just what it sounds like: The cat is unable to flee and has entered the fight mode. You will need to let the cat calm down over several hours.

Pain Aggression

If a normally nonaggressive cat lashes out at you, it is likely a pain issue. Cats are masters of hiding pain, so being familiar with the Feline Grimace Scale can help you recognize the symptoms. If your cat might be in pain, you will need to take them to the vet.

Idiopathic Aggression

This is a form of aggression for which no behavior or medical cause can be found. It is at this point that very difficult decisions need to be made. Surrendering a cat to a shelter with idiopathic aggression is unsafe for the shelter or potential adopters. Living with a cat like this can be dangerous for you. Thankfully these types of cases are rare.

ANXIETY AND FEAR

Anxiety in cats can be very complex. A cat's personality is shaped within the first few weeks of life through socialization. The cat's genetics plus a lack of socialization can result in an anxious cat.

A cat with anxiety is likely to have some level of chronic stress. This can cause hiding or fleeing from everyday events, and just as in humans, it can cause physiological changes leading to illness. Anxiety issues in cats generally surface between 12 to 36 months of age and progresses if left untreated. Let's look at some anxiety behaviors and how behavior modification can help.

Separation Anxiety

No one is quite sure why some cats have separation anxiety and others don't. Experts suspect that it can be caused by early weaning, genetics, boredom, or in some cases health issues. Separation anxiety manifests itself in several ways.

Remember the story of Harris, the cat with separation anxiety, in chapter 1? Harris's separation anxiety manifested as aggression. Your cat's separation anxiety may manifest by the cat urinating on your bed while you are on vacation or yowling at the window all day while you are at work. Your pet sitter may note a lack of appetite when you are away. These are all indications of separation anxiety.

Your vet might suggest medications that can help. It is important to understand that your cat is actually suffering. However, not every cat will need medication. You might have good results by using music therapy, installing calming pheromone diffusers, leaving your dirty clothes in the cat's favorite resting places, putting on some nightlights, and/or using puzzle feeders and timed treat dispensers to keep your cat busy. You could also try asking the pet sitter to come in the evening instead of the morning to help normalize the home while you are gone. If your cat sitter gets along well with your cat, you can ask if they would consider sleeping overnight. Dog sitters do overnights all the time for dogs, so why not have your sitter stay overnight with your cat?

Phobias

Yes, cats can have phobias. A phobia for an animal is anything that triggers a persistent anxiety response. Both dogs and cats can become anxious during thunderstorms, for example. If the stimulus causing the phobia can be removed (not easy with a thunderstorm, of course), I suggest removing it. Otherwise, you may need to desensitize your cat to whatever is causing the phobia.

It's helpful to give your cat areas to which they can escape, such as cat trees, tunnels, or perches where they can feel safe and observe their surroundings. You can also set up a safe refuge with a pheromone diffuser and some white noise in a bedroom or basement area. I do not recommend using a loud television to try and drown out thunderstorms, machinery, and other noises that might frighten your cat because the programs might include other loud noises like sirens, explosions, and car chases. I also don't recommend using cat music when dealing with phobias involving noises like thunderstorms or fireworks; white noise has a much better dampening effect. Once your cat goes to their refuge, you should leave them alone and let them determine when to come out of hiding.

Fear

Fear is an instinctual response to a perceived threat. Fear is different from anxiety because it is a reaction to something in the immediate environment, whereas anxiety is worry about a possible event. Fear is considered a normal response to real danger. Abnormal fear is a learned response from the cat's earlier experience. If someone in the household kicked the cat, the cat might develop a fear of that person; if the cat was abused by a man, any new man might trigger the freeze, fight, or flight response.

Abnormal fear responses can be unlearned, but it takes time and patience. We use counterconditioning techniques, where we replace the negative behavior with a positive response. An example would be having your male friend start feeding the cat their meals, so the cat learns that "this man is not a threat to me and good things happen when he is around." Another example would be a cat's learned fear of children. If this is the case, the children can be taught to properly engage with the cat using treats and interactive toys, with the goal of convincing the cat that they are not a threat.

It is important in learned fear cases not to force the cat to do anything they don't want to do. This may mean you need to keep your counterconditioning sessions less than five minutes long in the beginning, so you can win the cat's trust. Reaching for the cat, grabbing at the cat, or pulling the cat out of their hiding place only reinforces their fear.

ATTENTION-SEEKING BEHAVIOR

There can be several reasons for attention-seeking behavior, from medical issues to problems with the cat's environment and routine. As long as there is no underlying medical problem, cats with attention-seeking behavior benefit greatly from having a set routine of feeding, play, and environmental enrichments, with self-rewarding food puzzles and puzzle toys and perching areas so they can see outside. Ignoring the behavior simply isn't enough; you must fill in other areas of your cat's routine and stay on routine as much as possible.

Let's look at some common attention-seeking behaviors and how you might address them.

Howling at the Moon

Senior cats are the most likely to display this annoying behavior. You are in bed at night and you hear your cat meowing loudly and persistently. You get up to go check on them but there appears to be no obvious reason for the behavior. It calls for a trip to the vet.

Your cat might be suffering from hyperthyroidism or feline hyperesthesia, loss of eyesight, or some level of cognitive dysfunction.

If the vet finds nothing to indicate a medical cause of the behavior, there are several things you can try. Increase interactive playtime to at least twice a day. You can also scatter discovery treats throughout the house before bedtime. Set up food puzzles or treat balls before you go to bed to create the hunt, eat, groom, and sleep rhythm. When your cat wakes up in the early morning hours, they will roam around the house before beginning their noisy meowing. If you have staged food puzzles the night before, they will quietly hunt in the early dawn hours and be less likely to seek attention from you.

Insistent Meowing

Some cats, like the Siamese, are naturally chatty. If you like a chatty cat, feel free to talk to your cat. Both of you will enjoy the conversation. But if a cat that is not normally chatty begins meowing insistently, they might be trying to tell you that something physical is happening with them. If there are no physical problems, you can ignore the meowing and pay attention to your cat when they are quiet. Reward the behavior you want and ignore the behavior you want the cat to stop.

Counter/Desk Suffering

If you are trying to cook or work at your office desk, a cat that is insistent on attention can be very annoying. It can be of help to you to teach your cat that they have a place to go and receive attention. Some people find that simply placing a cardboard box at the end of the desk or counter resolves the behavior.

CHEWING/PICA

Nothing gets the attention of a cat owner faster than a cat chewing on inappropriate items. That kind of chewing is considered a type of obsessive-compulsive behavior. The causes might include genetics, dental issues, stress, inadequate mental stimulation, missing nutrients in the cat's diet, or an inability to absorb certain nutrients.

Look first for a medical reason for the behavior, such as dental disease or lack of important nutrition. Then take steps to manage the environment. Put electric cords into cord keepers, put clothing away or into hampers, and store throw blankets where the cat cannot get to them.

Once you've cleared your home of things the cat might chew on, find ways to enrich the cat's environment with puzzle toys, perching locations, cat trees, and interactive play. Reduce stressors in the home. Providing your cat with daily interactive play, music therapy, and other sound-dampening tools can help. If you have more than one cat, look for signs of tension between them and make sure they each have places they can go to nap or hide.

Also add appropriate items for the cat to chew on. I am a big fan of indoor cat gardens. While we want to remove toxic plants from our cat's temptation, we can add plants that are safe and pleasing. Cat grass, rosemary, lemongrass, parsley, and basil are all great choices that both you and your cat can safely enjoy. Lily, my own cat, adores lemongrass, and I grow it year-round in a container garden along with rosemary and parsley. You can add catnip to the indoor cat garden because it is a mild sedative for cats when eaten.

COUNTER SURFING

Some owners don't mind a cat strutting across the kitchen counter, while other owners do not want Ms. Litter Paws up there. If the cat is counter surfing it is because you are leaving food items out. If this issue is a true attention-seeking behavior, we can address this through training and counterconditioning.

» Remove all food items from the counter.
» Use a passive deterrent on the counter, such as an upside-down carpet protector with the spikey side up or motion-activated spray pet deterrent.

» Train the cat to go to a certain spot on or near the counter. The cat wants to be up high, observing the kitchen activity. You can use a barstool or a designated cat pad or box.
» If your cat likes to get up on the counter to access the drip from the kitchen tap, provide your cat a trickle fountain of their own. The keyword is trickle, not slide nor waterfall.

OVERGROOMING

Let's have a word here about fleas. Yes, even your indoor cat can get fleas. Flea eggs can remain viable in the environment for months, and if picked up on your shoes, your child's clothing, your dog, or an outdoor cat, those eggs can end up on your carefully sheltered indoor cat, leading to overgrooming in an attempt to get rid of the parasites.

Overgrooming can also be an allergic reaction to something in the environment or the food; in that case, a veterinary allergist can help develop a treatment plan. Similarly, a cat may be grooming an area that is painful or one that is just out of reach.

Finally, overgrooming can be caused by stress in the cat's environment, such as loud noises, tension with other cats, a new environment, or a new person, especially a new baby.

LOUD NOISES

» Loud noises can be mitigated with sound dampening or cat music.

TENSION WITH OTHER CATS

» Recognize the signs of inter-cat aggression: cats staring each other down, spraying or marking territory, or other resource guarding of food and litter boxes.
» Use of a modified reintroduction plan like an initial cat introduction.

NEW ENVIRONMENT

» Introduce your cat slowly to a new environment.
» Try using calming pheromone diffusers.
» When moving to a new residence, keep some of the old cat beds until your cat has settled into their new home.

NEW PERSON IN THE ENVIRONMENT

» Have an introduction plan of feeding and interactive play with the new person.

ARRIVAL OF A NEW BABY

» Prepare your cat six to eight weeks in advance.
» Introduce the cat to the nursery.
» Establish the cat's own go-to bed in the nursery.
» Play recordings of normal baby sounds. Borrow items with a baby's scent on them from friends.
» Ask a friend to bring their baby over so the cat can see and hear them. This also gives you a good opportunity to gauge how your cat will react when you bring your own baby home.

TRAVELING WITH AND WITHOUT YOUR CAT

Traveling with your cat can be fun, or it can fraught with difficulties. Training your cat to love their carrier helps make the trip go smoothly. But you can't always take your cat with you, so you also need to prepare for the times when you need to leave them behind.

Using a Cat Carrier

Teaching your cat to love their carrier is one of the best things you can do for the cat, yourself, and, surprisingly, for your veterinarian and groomer! Cats trained to love their carriers show up at the vet office less stressed and much easier to handle, and you'll need to use the carrier whenever you take your cat somewhere with you. Here are the steps to go about changing a recalcitrant cat's attitude about the dreaded carrier:

1. Disassemble the carrier and leave only the bottom of the carrier in the room with the cat. The goal is to have the bottom become their new bed over the next week or so.
2. Train your cat to use a specific bed or blanket that is not in the crate bottom.
3. Move the bed or blanket into the carrier bottom. Reward the cat for going to it.
4. Put the lid on the carrier without the door. When you see your cat using the carrier as a resting place, reinforce this behavior with a reward.
5. Add the carrier door but leave it open. Continue to reward the cat for going into the carrier.
6. Close the carrier door while the cat is in the carrier and reward them with treats through the door. Leave the door closed for only seven to eight seconds at first. Continue to work on increasing the duration over the next few weeks.
7. Once the cat can stay happily in the carrier, try lifting the crate up and placing it back down. Again, reward your cat for the activity. Increase the time until you can bring the carrier to the car.
8. Place the carrier in the car, give the cat a treat through the carrier door, and take them back to the house. Eventually you will take your cat for a car ride around the block and back home.

Finding a Good Pet Sitter or Boarding Facility

You can't always—nor would you want to—take your cat along when you travel. Unless you have a friend who can care for the cat while you're away, you'll need a cat sitter. It can be hard to locate a good sitter and introduce the sitter to the cat, so be sure to start well ahead of time.

The best place to start is with a phone call to your veterinary office. Many offices maintain a small list of trusted local pet sitters. If your vet doesn't have such a list, you will need to do a bit more homework. Look for a professional pet sitter, or a cat sitting company dedicated to cat care if there's one in your area. Contact possible sitters or companies and conduct a phone interview. Ask about the following:

» Bonding, insurance, years in business, and affiliations such as veterinary offices, rescues, or professional pet sitting organizations.
» How they interact with cats (I think this is very important to discuss on the phone before scheduling a meet and greet).
» How they would handle a frightened or sick cat, and what they would do to address separation anxiety.
» Are their visits express cat visits with just food, water, and scooping cat litter, or do they spend time playing with the cat?

Before inviting a potential pet sitter over for a meet and greet, look for online reviews on Google, Facebook, Yelp, and other review sites. Don't go by the stars. Read the reviews to see if they address things like how well the sitter or the company does with cats and how knowledgeable they are about cats. If all you see is how great they are with dogs, look elsewhere. Once you are satisfied with a potential pet sitter, invite them over for an introduction to your cat, a home tour, and a key exchange.

If you find yourself needing to board your cat instead of using a sitter, start by asking your veterinarian's office for recommendations. Visit possible boarding facilities to see the boarding area for cats. Ask what is and is not included in their fee. Some boarding facilities charge a cuddle time fee, and if you don't pay it, your cat isn't going to get much attention. Ask whether they have environmental enrichment for the cats. One facility near me has a giant fish tank next to glass-enclosed cat condos and individually circulated air to limit the spread of bacteria between cats. Their boarding fee is only slightly higher than that of a top pet sitter. If you need to board your cat, it is well worth paying more so your cat doesn't end up with a windowless steel cage, barking dogs nearby, and little attention other than feeding and scooping.

ESCAPING THE HOUSE

When you leave the house, your cat might want to leave, too. They might even try to leave every time the door is opened. Door dashing, which is when your cat makes attempts to dash out the door at every opportunity, is a dangerous habit. Indoor cats can experience sensory overload in the outdoor environment, be injured by other cats or wildlife, be exposed to parasites or diseases, or be hit or injured by a car.

Like so many other unwanted behaviors, one solution to door dashing is to enrich your indoor cat's environment. When you leave the house, make sure your cat has an interesting activity, such as busy box toys and activity boards, to engage with while you are away. Spending a few minutes in interactive play with your cat before you leave and when you return can also be helpful.

Establish a specific area for greetings and departures. Set up an area, preferably a cat tree away from the door or in another room altogether. When you get ready to leave, call your cat to the cat tree and reward them with treats or a food puzzle, then proceed to calmly walk out the door. When returning home, open the door slowly and walk to the cat tree to greet your cat and give them a treat. Eventually, your cat will associate your departure and return with the specific spot.

If your cat is particularly persistent about trying to get out, you can use passive deterrents like Sticky Paws on the floor in front of the door or motion-activated air cans that release a hiss of air if the cat gets too close. But remember not to use a deterrent without having a positive alternative. If nothing else works and you have a garage attached to your house, you can use what I call an air lock. Instead of using the door to the street, exit and enter your house through the garage, being sure to close the garage door after you.

Finding Your Lost Cat

If by chance your door dasher makes the great escape, there are a few things you can do and a few things to keep in mind. First, indoor-only cats usually do not go very far, perhaps staying within a five to seven house range during the first few days.

You need to understand that your cat is frightened and will be hiding. Your best time to locate them is at dawn or dusk. To tempt the cat home, place your dirty clothing on your porch or back patio, and put their bed in a sheltered area outside. Your cat will stay close to that scent. Some people even recommend putting a dirty litter box outside. The thinking is that your cat doesn't have a marked territory, so this might help to keep them in the local area. But if you have a large stray cat population, the litter box may attract aggressive tomcats to your yard, chasing your cat further away from home.

Let your neighbors and people in the area know that your cat has escaped by talking with them or posting flyers asking anyone who sees the cat to get in touch with you. Having a collar on your cat with your contact information may be helpful if someone finds them. If your cat is microchipped, be sure the information is up-to-date. When you finally find your cat, don't go running toward them. Instead, use treats, canned food, or tuna fish to convince them to come to you.

CHAPTER TEN

TRAINING AND TRICKS

T raining is a great way to improve your bond with your cat, to teach them good household manners, and to become an Internet sensation. Okay, maybe the last one isn't guaranteed, but you can certainly post fun videos.

Cat training is like a magical door that opens onto communication and trust between cat and owner. The cat pictured with me in my author photo is Lucy. The photographer was so impressed with her confidence in his studio that he wanted her to stay and be his studio cat. He had photographed thousands of dogs and a few cats, and Lucy was the first to not get freaked out by being in this new place. This was because Lucy has been thoroughly trained.

THE BASICS OF TRAINING

Dogs get all the training glory, but cats can be trained, too! You just have to understand what motivates their behavior. Many cat owners feel as if they are on their own when it comes to training because there are no cat behavior consultants in their area, but many behavior consultants and trainers offer virtual consultations. If you are having trouble, you can reach out to them via phone, Facetime, Skype, or Zoom.

The important thing to remember about cat training is that it is a huge lesson in positive reinforcement training, because cats don't respond to negative punishments. Positive reinforcement training means taking opportunities to reward the behavior you want and offering the cat better alternative choices for behavior you do not want.

Below you'll find detailed steps about how to do various types of training, including clicker training.

Clicker Training

Most dog people have heard of clicker training, but cats also respond to this style of training quite well. In fact, I have found anecdotally that cats respond to clicker training very quickly if good things happen when they hear the clicker. When you say positive words like "good girl," your tone or inflection can give the cat mixed signals; also, these words may be used in various situations that fail to provide a reinforcer like a treat. A clicker is more consistent.

There are two types of clicker training: operant training and classical training. Let's look at these two techniques a bit more closely, and then I will give you some lessons to help you learn how to use the clicker to change your cat's behavior.

Operant training is opportunity training. The cat presents you with a desired behavior, and you have the opportunity to reinforce the behavior. Classical training, also called classical conditioning, is much like Pavlov's dogs who learned to drool every time the bell rang. Classical conditioning depends on a natural reflexive response to a stimulus.

Using a clicker in training is a form of two-way communication with your cat. You and your cat learn what to expect from each other in a way that is fun for both of you and naturally reinforces the bond between you. Not only will your cat learn something new, you will feel less frustrated and the environment in the home will be happier for everyone.

Be sure that the rewards you give for positive behavior are of sufficient value to your cat. Your clicker is a conditioning tool and the high-value reward is the reinforcer.

One last thing about clicker training: Some cats are frightened by the loud sound of dog clickers. If that is the case with your cat, you can use a tool called a soft clicker, a pen that clicks when you open or close it, or even a tongue knock. Whatever tool you choose needs to be easy for you to use consistently.

PRACTICE USING THE CLICKER

In this lesson you'll learn how to use the clicker. This lesson may seem silly at first glance, but it is important that you get comfortable with the tool. Clicker training is about watching for the desired behavior, clicking when the cat exhibits the behavior, and rapidly rewarding the behavior. If you fumble with the clicker or the treat, you will give the cat mixed messages.

TO PRACTICE USING THE CLICKER, YOU WILL NEED:

Clicker

Treat bag or container

Treats

Full length mirror or the ability to record yourself on your phone

1. Practice holding the clicker and clicking. Try it in both hands, because during training you will use one hand to click and the other to deliver a reward rapidly.

2. Practice holding the clicker as still as possible. I like to hold the clicker behind my back, but you might like it at your side or waist. The point is to keep the body still during the click.

3. Practice clicking and at the same time placing a treat on the floor in front of you. If you keep fumbling your treat bag or container, consider changing to one that is easier for you.

4. Once you think you have the actions down, watch yourself in the mirror or record yourself doing a rapid click/reward 10 times in succession. Look for excess body movements and any fumbling with the clicker or treats. Continue to work on your skills until you have improved so they are not distracting.

CHARGING THE CLICKER AND YOUR CAT

You can use the clicker in classical conditioning to help your cat make the association between the clicker and the reward. This entire lesson shouldn't take more than two to three minutes to complete. Practice this twice a day.

THINGS YOU WILL NEED FOR THIS EXERCISE:

Clicker

High-value treat

Quiet room

1. Place your cat in the quiet room or area.

2. Sit or stand in front of your cat and click and deliver treats in rapid succession. As soon as your cat finishes one treat, click and provide another.

3. Watch for your cat to start looking for the click or at you. Click and reward when this behavior begins. You have moved from classical conditioning to operant training, and your cat is ready to offer you opportunities to reward behaviors.

4. Put the treats and clicker away. You are done with the lesson.

COME WHEN CALLED

This valuable lesson is one that can get your cat out of danger, help find them if they dart out the door, and locate them if they are hiding. Most cats will already show up when they hear the treat bag rustle, so what we are really doing is putting that behavior on a cue so we can use the clicker in other circumstances. Keep the training sessions short. About five minutes twice a day is enough.

THINGS YOU WILL NEED FOR THIS EXERCISE:

Clicker

High-value treats

Quiet room

1. Place your cat in a quiet area.

2. Provide two or three clicks and rewards to charge the session.

3. Move away from your cat.

4. When your cat begins to walk toward you, say your cat's name, click, and give them a treat.

5. Once your cat is responding well in the quiet room, start practicing in other areas around the home that have more distractions.

6. Eventually, replace the treats with head scratches and cheek rubs.

TARGETING

Teaching your cat a targeting behavior helps you shape other behaviors—such as leading them to their cat tree, a veterinary exam table, or other locations. I used targeting with Lucy in the photographer's studio when she wandered out of the shot.

For targeting training, you can use a target stick with a built-in clicker, your finger, or a simple tool—I have even used a wooden spoon or Popsicle stick. Practice the steps below for a few minutes several times a day.

THINGS YOU WILL NEED FOR THIS EXERCISE:

Clicker

High-value treats

Target stick or other tool

1. Place your cat in front of you.

2. Offer the target to your cat.

3. When your cat moves to sniff the target, click and reward.

4. Once your cat is consistently moving toward the target or touching it with their nose, start offering the target in different positions.

5. Move farther away from your cat. When they start to move toward the target, click and reward, using the verbal cue "target."

6. Continue to create distance between your cat and the target, clicking and rewarding your cat when they move toward the target.

7. Make a slow circle around your cat, offering the target and pausing to click and reward them as they turn toward the target. Put this behavior on cue by saying "spin."

GO TO BOX/MAT

Go to box is useful if you need your cat to go to a certain location and stay there. You will use this exercise for all your departures or arrivals home. This is an excellent exercise if you have a door dasher! The box type I recommend is the canned cat food tray from a case of cat food, which you can get for free from any pet food supply store. You can also use a small towel, mat, or cat bed.

THINGS YOU WILL NEED FOR THIS EXERCISE:

Clicker

High-value treat

Box (or other place for the cat to lie down)

1. Call your cat to come to you. Click and reward.

2. Place the box on the floor between you and your cat.

3. Let your cat sniff the box. Click and reward.

4. If your cat puts one paw in the box, click and reward by tossing the treat outside the box. You may be tempted to lure them into the box, but at this point you want your cat to offer the behavior and give you the opportunity to reward them. You can also use your target stick to get this behavior started by having them target in the box.

5. Once your cat is successfully putting one paw in the box, wait to click until they have two front paws in the box. Then click and reward.

6. Continue building on this exercise until your cat is fully sitting in the box.

7. Create some distance between you and the box and cue your cat to "go to box." Once your cat is in the box, wait a few seconds and then click and reward by tossing the treats away from the box. Start with a few seconds. Gradually increase the time they need to wait, with the goal of getting them to wait for a few minutes.

8. Move the box to other locations around your home and ask your cat to "go to box." Have them wait in the box and then click and toss treats away from the box.

9. Once your cat knows to "go to box," use this behavior to be able to walk out the door without the cat dashing to get through. For example, you can ask your cat to go to box, wait, place rewards on the floor, and then click as you walk out the door.

10. When returning, immediately ask your cat to "go to box" and click/reward. It will take some time, but your cat will learn that good things happen if they stay in the box when you come and go, rather than darting out the door.

COME ALONG

Once your cat has mastered targeting behavior, use it to teach them to "come along." This behavior is helpful when you need your cat to come with you to a certain location. The come along exercise builds trust between you and your cat by teaching them that you won't take them anywhere dangerous. You can use it when you do harness training to walk your cat outside or to bring the cat back if they should dart out the door.

THINGS YOU WILL NEED FOR THIS EXERCISE:

Clicker   Target stick

High-value treats

1. Call your cat to come to you. Click and reward.

2. Hold the target at your side at about knee height and say "target." Click and reward.

3. Turn your back to your cat and take three steps away from them, with the target remaining at your knee. Say "target." Click and reward. Take three more steps away and repeat. Continue until the cat is following you.

4. Repeat step 3, changing the cue word to "come along" or "follow." Have your cat come along with you to different locations in the house.

UP/DOWN

Teaching your cat up and down is both useful and fun. When used to address counter surfing, your cat will learn that that the countertop is a no reward zone. Conversely, they learn where they can go up, like the sofa, your lap, or the windowsill. Remember that when you discourage one behavior like leaping onto the countertop, you need to replace it with an alternative behavior.

THINGS YOU WILL NEED FOR THIS EXERCISE:

Clicker

High-value treats

Cat tree

Target stick

1. Start slow and work with a low cat tree first. Using your target stick, say "target" while pointing at the top of the cat tree. Click and reward, using the cue "up." Some cats enjoy the "up" and they will perform it just to receive attention from you. Practice "up" until your cat does it on cue.

2. Hold your target stick on the floor and cue the word "down." If the cat jumps down, click and reward.

3. Once the cat responds to the up/down cues at the cat tree, add a third location and practice cueing your cat to go up, down, and up again. When the cat responds to the cue, click and reward.

4. We want to ignore the unwanted behavior of surfing for attention and have the cat get down and then go to the third location. This might be a barstool or low cat tree in the kitchen, where they can observe and not be in the way. I have at least one client that has their cat actually go up on top of the cabinets as their alternative location. You might decide "go to box" on a corner of the counter works as well.

SIT PRETTY

Building on some of the skills you have already learned, you can teach your cat to Sit Pretty. This little show-off trick is fun.

THINGS YOU WILL NEED FOR THIS EXERCISE:

Clicker

Target stick

High-value Treats

1. Call your cat to come to you. Click and reward.

2. Wait for the cat to sit on its own. Click and reward by tossing the treat away from you.

3. Call the cat again. When they come back to you, wait for the cat to sit, then cue the word "sit." Click and reward, again by tossing the treat away from you.

4. Once your cat is sitting consistently, hold your target stick high over their head. Your cat should sit up or start to reach up to the target. Click and reward. Start using the cue "sit pretty."

5. Once your cat is consistently sitting or sitting pretty, fade the use of the clicker and reward.

6. Sit and Sit Pretty can be tedious tricks to learn, so keep sessions brief. Practice several times a day.

HIGH FIVE

This is another fun trick for you and your cat. It is generally easy to teach.

THINGS YOU WILL NEED FOR THIS EXERCISE:

Clicker   High-value treats

1. Sit on the floor in front of your cat with a treat in your closed fist. Hold your fist out at the height of the cat's shoulder.

2. When your cat puts their paw on your fist, click and give the treat.

3. Repeat several times until your cat consistently puts their paw on your fist when you hold it out.

4. If your cat doesn't reach with their paw for the treat, start with your fist at floor level and let them paw at your hand. Gradually work up to the cat's shoulder level.

5. When your cat responds consistently, start offering your hand palm up without the treat.

6. Click and reward with your other hand when your cat puts their paw in your hand.

HARNESS TRAINING FOR THE ADVENTUROUS

This training is for the well-accomplished cat owner and cat. You and your cat should be very comfortable with each other, coming when called and targeting. Not every cat will enjoy wearing a harness and going for a walk—some cats find it a terrifying experience. Don't force your cat into this activity. They might slip out of the harness and run off. But if your cat takes to harness training, both of you can enjoy strolling through a garden or taking a quiet nature walk.

THINGS YOU WILL NEED FOR THIS EXERCISE:

Cat harness

Leash

High-value treats

Large towel or tote bag

1. Begin by simply introducing the harness to your cat. Leave it near the feeding station and let your cat sniff it for several days.

2. Put the harness on your cat, but leave it unfastened. Reward your cat with food or treats while they wear it. Keep these sessions short and practice this for several days until your cat is comfortable wearing the harness.

3. Fasten the harness and adjust the fit. The fit should allow for two fingers under the harness. Remember that cats can back out of most harnesses if they become frightened. Your cat may freeze at this point or fall over or walk oddly. Just reward, reward, reward. Keep sessions short and allow your cat to become accustomed to the feel of wearing the harness indoors.

4. After a week or so, attach the leash and let it drag on the floor. Let your cat get used to the feel of the harness with the leash. Walking a cat is not at all like walking a dog. The cat calls the shots, so we want them to feel comfortable in their new gear. Using a teaser wand toy can help them adjust.

5. When your cat is comfortable wearing the harness with the leash in the house, pick them up and carry them outside. Always carry your cat. Do not let them walk out on their own or you might encourage door dashing.

6. Keep outdoor sessions short and rewarding, making sure that if your cat becomes startled, they have a way to run back inside or you have a towel to put over them so you can carry them back inside. I used to always carry a large cloth tote bag for my one adventurous cat. When she became uncomfortable or I saw a dog heading our way, she had the option of hopping in the tote bag.

RESOURCES

BOOKS

Show Biz Tricks for Cats: 30 Fun and Easy Tricks You Can Teach Your Cat by Anne Gordon and Steve Duno. Adams Media, 1996.

Think Like a Cat: How to Raise a Well-Adjusted Cat—Not a Sour Puss by Pam Johnson-Bennett. Penguin, 2000.

Understanding Cat Behavior by Roger Tabor. David & Charles, 2003.

WEBSITES

American College of Veterinary Behaviorists
dacvb.org
This is a certifying board of veterinarians involved in the research of behavior education and the practice of clinical behavioral medicine in animals.

Cat Fanciers' Association
cfa.org
While the CFA's signature is the cat show, they also have a pedigree of other programs supporting the care of cats. These programs include an Ambassador Program, Animal Welfare Committee including TNR (Train, Neuter, and Release), Breeders Assistance Program, Feline Agility, Mentoring, The Winn Foundation, and Youth Feline Education Program. No other organization does more for the health and welfare of ALL cats than the CFA. I highly encourage you to check them out.

Fear Free Happy Homes

fearfreehappyhomes.com

Their mission is to alleviate fear, anxiety, and stress in pets by inspiring and educating the people who care for them.

International Association of Animal Behavior Consultants

iaabc.org

IAABC members believe in the study and science of behavior consulting. We understand that animal behavior consultants can assist owners in managing and modifying problem behaviors, and in the process help strengthen the relationship between an owner and pet. Many consultants offer virtual consultations with you and your pet.

Professional Cat Groomers Association

professionalcatgroomers.com

Finding a professional cat groomer can be a challenge because it takes a special person who understands your cat's temperament, personality, and needs. Certified Master Cat Groomers have gone beyond the basics and have achieved the highest level of certification. These elite groomers have a deeper understanding and appreciation of felines.

REFERENCES

CHAPTERS ONE THROUGH THREE

Brulliard, Karin. "Cats Do Have Facial Expressions, but You Probably Can't Read Them." *The Washington Post* (blog). November 30, 2019. Washingtonpost.com/science/2019/11/30/cats-do-have-facial -expressions-you-probably-cant-read-them.

Evangelista, Marina C., Ryota Watanabe, Vivian S. Y. Leung, Beatriz P. Monteiro, Elizabeth O'Toole, Daniel S. J. Pang, and Paulo V. Steagall. "Facial Expressions of Pain in Cats: the Development and Validation of a Feline Grimace Scale." *Scientific Reports* 9, no. 19128 (December 13, 2019). Doi.org/10.1038/s41598-019-55693-8.

Heffner, Rickye S. and Henry Heffner. "Hearing Range of the Domestic Cat." *Hearing Research* 19, no. 1 (February 1985): 85–88. Doi.org/10.1016/0378-5955(85)90100-5.

Lyons, Leslie A. "Why Do Cats Purr?" *Scientific American*. Last modified April 3, 2006. ScientificAmerican.com/article/why-do-cats-purr.

Muir, Hazel. "Ancient Remains Could Be Oldest Pet Cat." *New Scientist*. April 8, 2004. NewScientist.com/article/dn4867-ancient -remains-could-be-oldest-pet-cat.

Ollila, Erin. "Differences Between Dogs and Cats: Learn What Makes Each One Special." *Hill's Pet Nutrition*. November 16, 2016. HillsPet.com/pet-care/resources/differences-between-cats -and-dogs.

Peterson, Michael E., and Michelle Anne Kutzler. *Small Animal Pediatrics: The First 12 Months of Life*. St. Louis, MO: Saunders, 2011.

"Spay/Neuter Your Pet." ASPCA. Accessed June 17, 2020. https:// www.aspca.org/pet-care/general-pet-care/spayneuter-your-pet.

CHAPTERS FOUR THROUGH SEVEN

ASPCA. "Poisonous Plants." Accessed March 12, 2020. ASPCA.org /pet-care/animal-poison-control/toxic-and-non-toxic-plants.

Delgado, Mikel and Julie Hecht. "A Review of the Development and Functions of Cat Play, with Future Research Considerations." *Applied Animal Behaviour Science* 214 (May 2019): 1–17. Doi.org /10.1016/j.applanim.2019.03.004.

Drake Center for Veterinary Care. "Catnip and Your Cat—What It Is, What It Does, Why It Doesn't Affect All Cats." Accessed January 23, 2020. TheDrakeCenter.com/services/cats/blog/catnip-and-your -cat-what-it-what-it-does-and-why-it-doesn't-affect-all-cats.

Food Puzzles for Cats. FoodPuzzlesforCats.com. Accessed January 22, 2020.

Hewson-Hughes, Adrian K., Victoria L. Hewson-Hughes, Andrew T. Miller, Simon R. Hall, Stephen J. Simpson, and David Raubenheimer. "Geometric Analysis of Macronutrient Selection in the Adult Domestic Cat, *Felis Catus*." *Journal of Experimental Biology* 214 (2011): 1039–1051. Doi.org/10.1242/jeb.049429.

Lombardi, Linda. "What Current Science Tells Us About Cat Play." *Fear Free Pets*. September 27, 2019. FearFreePets.com/science-of-cat-play.

Miller, Kelli. "How to Read Cat Food Labels: Eight Tips for Deciphering Cat Food Names and Claims." *Fetch by WebMD* (blog). May 4, 2010. Pets.WebMD.com/cats/guide/how-to-read-cat-food-labels#1.

"Obesity." Cornell University College of Veterinary Medicine, May 22, 2018. Vet.Cornell.edu/departments-centers -and-institutes/cornell-feline-health-center/health-information /feline-health-topics/obesity.

Pasek, Beth. "Yes You Can Have Plants and Cats." *Finicky* (blog). Finicky.us/cat-care-tips-1/f/yes-you-can-have-plants-and-cats.

Rowlands, Richard. "The Best Cat Toothpastes (2020 Reviews)." Cat Life Today. Last modified June 9, 2020. CatLifeToday.com/best-cat -toothpastes.

Waltham Petcare Science Institute. "A Game of Cat and Mouse." Accessed February 1, 2020. Waltham.com/news-events/nutrition /a-game-of-cat-and-mouse/5549.

CHAPTERS EIGHT THROUGH TEN

American Veterinary Medical Association. "Welfare Implications of Declawing of Domestic Cats." July 23, 2019. AVMA.org /resources-tools/literature-reviews/welfare-implications-declawing -domestic-cats.

Cornell University College of Veterinary Medicine. "Feline Behavior Problems: Aggression." Last modified December 2016. Vet.cornell .edu/departments-centers-and-institutes/cornell-feline-health-center /health-information/feline-health-topics/feline-behavior-problems -aggression.

German, Alex. "Extreme Fear and Anxiety in Cats." PetMD. February 5, 2010. PetMD.com/cat/conditions/behavioral /c_ct_fear_phobia_anxiety.

Johnson, Ingrid. "Redirected Aggression in Cats: Recognition and Treatment Strategies." International Association of Animal Behavior Consultants. May 17, 2014. IAABC.org/cat/redirected-aggression -in-cats.

Martell-Moran, Nicole K., Mauricio Solano, and Hugh GG Townsend. "Pain and Adverse Behavior in Declawed Cats." *Journal of Feline Medicine and Surgery* 20, no. 4 (May 23, 2017): 280–88. Doi.org /10.1177/1098612X17705044.

INDEX

A

Actions, 22–23
Adolescent cats, 4
Adult cats, 4
Aggression, 20, 93–97
American shorthairs, 9
American Veterinary Medical
    Association (AVMA), 84
Anxiety, 7, 97–98
Attention-seeking, 99–100

B

Behavior
    by age, 3–5
    vs. dog behavior, 10–11
    indoor vs. outdoor, 12
    modification, 92
    by sex, 5–6
Bengal cats, 8
Boarding facilities, 104–105
Breeds, 8–9

C

Carriers, 3, 103–104
Cat Fanciers', Association, 8
Catnip, 42
Chewing, 100–101
Children, 33–34
Classical training, 110
Clicker training, 110–113
Communication
    body language, 21–23
    facial expressions, 17–19
    from humans, 23–24
    noises, 16–17
    play-related, 23, 44–46
Counter surfing, 100, 101–102

D

Declawing, 84–85
Dental care, 53
Dogs, 10–11, 34–36
Domestication, 2–3
Door dashing, 106–107

E

Ears, 18–19
Elimination, 74. *See also* Litter boxes
Escaping, 106–107
Evolution, 2
Eyes, 17–18

F

Fatty liver syndrome, 71
Fear, 96, 98–99
Feather wands, 40
Feline Grimace Scale, 19
Females, 6
Flehmening, 23
Food
    aggression, 93–94
    feeding frequency, 60, 64
    human, 66
    labels, 69–70
    picky eating, 59, 68–70

ACKNOWLEDGMENTS

I would like to acknowledge the kind words of support and encouragement from Sharman Soeder, one of my very first cat care clients. Her enthusiasm for me to share my knowledge cannot be understated.

I would like to thank Callisto Media for the opportunity to write this book, which without their efforts would have never come to completion.

ABOUT THE AUTHOR

BETH PASEK is the owner of Finicky Cat Sitting and Behavior, LLC. In 2020, the organization celebrated 10 years in the pet care industry as a multiyear award-winning pet sitting and animal behavior company for both cats and dogs. She has worked with several rescues as a volunteer cat behavior consultant for special needs diabetic cats in transition and has provided a foster home for kittens and critical care cats. She is a supporting member of both the International Association of Animal Behavior Consultants-Cat Division and the International Association of Animal Hospice and Palliative Care. Her ongoing coursework includes certification through Karen Pryor Academy's Train Your Cat.

Printed in the USA
CPSIA information can be obtained
at www.ICGtesting.com
LVHW050134060724
784546LV00006B/15